Miraculous Healing

A Personal Testimony and Biblical Study.

HENRY W. FROST

ZONDERVAN
PUBLISHING HOUSE
OF THE ZONDERVAN CORPORATION | GRAND RAPIDS, MICHIGAN 49506

MIRACULOUS HEALING
Copyright © 1972 by Overseas Missionary Fellowship
Foreword © 1979 by The Zondervan Corporation

Published by The Zondervan Corporation by special arrangement with
Overseas Missionary Fellowship, Belmont, Kent, England. Zondervan
edition first published 1979.

Library of Congress Cataloging in Publication Data

Frost, Henry Weston, 1858-
  Miraculous healing.

  Reprint of the 1972 ed. published by Evangelical Press, London; with new
foreword.
  1. Faith-cure—Case studies.   2.   Jesus Christ—
Miracles.   I.   Title.
BT732.5.F73 1979   231'.73   79-11921
ISBN 0-310-38291-2

Printed in the United States of America

CONTENTS

FOREWORD

Just about every morning around our house my sister Jay goes through a daily routine of coaxing her reluctant handicapped sister out of dreamland and into a new day. "Swoosh" go the curtains—and in rush impatient rays of sunlight to pounce on my sleepy eyelids. If that doesn't work, reinforcements must be sent in. "Click" goes the TV knob—and out pour the loud, cheery sounds of a morning talk show (very unconducive to sleeping in).

I say "morning talk show," but if it's a Sunday morning there's often a TV preacher on instead. Sometimes there's a healing service on, and I will watch it as I am being exercised, dressed, made up, and lifted into my wheelchair. It's rather paradoxical to be sitting there, handicapped and unable to care for myself, listening to the sermon and watching people hobble onstage with crutches and walk off without them. "Jesus doesn't want you sick and disabled," the speaker will often say. "He wants to do for you what He's done for those you've seen today. You, too, can experience His healing power. Rest your faith on His promises."

As I watch I often think about other sick and handicapped people, all over the country, viewing the same broadcast. What are they thinking? Are they asking themselves the same questions I asked several years ago? Questions like, Does God still heal people miraculously today? If so, does He want to heal all or just some? And what am I to think if my prayers for healing go unanswered, unlike the prayers of those I see on TV?

One of the milestones for me in answering questions like these was the book you hold in your hands, *Miraculous Healing*, by Henry W. Frost. I wish that everyone who wonders about healing could read it. It's not a new book. In fact, the language is a bit turn of the century. But I doubt whether you will find a more sensible and balanced treatment anywhere.

Writing as an eyewitness, Mr. Frost examines situations where God *did* heal and then asks, Now what did all these people have, or do, in common? What keys can we find if we wish to be healed as well? His conclusions are not only helpful and interesting, but they confirm what he shows the Bible teaches. This double-edged sword of Scripture and personal experience cuts through thickets of error and misconception to present one of the clearest discussions about miraculous healing of which I know.

JONI EARECKSON

ENDORSEMENT

I AM truly glad that the publishers have decided to reprint this excellent volume, largely perhaps at my suggestion.

Ever since I first read it, I have felt that it is easily and incomparably the best book I have ever read on this subject. It is the book, therefore, which I have always recommended to those who have been anxious for help on this matter. Many times have I been asked to write myself on this theme. I have always replied by saying that Henry W. Frost has already dealt with the matter in what I regard as a final and conclusive manner.

The reappearance of this book at this present time is most opportune as there is evidently a recrudescence of interest in this subject.

Some recent writings seem to suggest that the only problem is as to whether one believes or not that miraculous gifts ended with the apostolic age. But this is by no means the only problem.

Dr. Frost shows clearly that theological problems are also involved, and which we only ignore at our spiritual peril. The Bible frequently warns us against the danger of being deluded by evil powers. All " miracles " and " wonders " are not produced by the Holy Spirit, and we must know how to " test the spirits " in this matter. Our Lord Himself has warned us that the " lying spirits " are so clever and so subtle as to deceive, if it were possible, the very elect (Matt. 24.24).

Dr. Frost's method is particularly helpful. He starts on the practical level by citing cases and examples which prove the fact of miraculous healing. He then proceeds to deal with the difficulties, both on the practical and experimental plane, and also in the realm of correct and clear thinking. Above all, he is thoroughly biblical, and not only orthodox, but truly spiritually-minded.

I strongly recommend this most valuable study.

D. M. LLOYD-JONES.

PREFACE

It will be noted that the title which I have chosen for this book is, "Miraculous Healing," instead of the usual phrase, "Divine Healing." This change of phraseology has been purposely made. The special theme of the book is God's healing apart from means, which the words " miraculous healing " indicate. But this would not be true of the words " divine healing," for these, properly understood, signify God's healing both without and with means. This last is the case because it is a fact that healing of any kind is necessarily divine. A physician does not heal, nor medicine, nor a scientific diet, nor an improved environment, nor anything else that may be named. All creation or recreation is from God; and hence, in every instance of healing He is the One who heals, whether He acts directly through unknown laws or indirectly through known laws. Where in this book, therefore, the words "divine healing" occur it is to be understood that any form of healing is signified, but where the words "miraculous healing" occur that only healing apart from means is signified.

It will be further noted that I have somewhat criticised parts of what Dr. A. J. Gordon and Dr. A. B. Simpson wrote upon the subject of miraculous healing. I have regretted the necessity of this. These men of God presented to Christians much truth concerning healing apart from means; and besides, their service as writers, preachers, teachers and missionary leaders was extensive and uniquely fruitful in blessing. It is, therefore, to be kept in mind, that my criticisms do not indicate any lack of esteem on my part for these beloved brethren. I greatly revere their memory and desire that others should do the same.

I

AN OPENING TESTIMONY

Just when in my early life I became a Christian, I do not know. As far as I can think backward, I have the remembrance of believing in Christ and of having some measure of desire to be His true disciple. The time, however, when I entered into the experience of assurance may easily and definitely be recalled. This was after I had left Princeton College, when I was living in Attica, in western New York, and was engaged in business. There, one memorable day, I was led to accept for myself the testimony of God's Word concerning the substitutionary work of Christ; and then learning the secret of fixing my faith, not upon inner evidence of any kind, but upon the great outward evidence of revealed and established truth, I entered into a rest, which, thank God! has never since been broken.

This experience of God's grace and love awakened in my heart an altogether new longing to know and understand the Holy Scriptures. It was a natural as well as a logical conclusion at which to arrive, that the Word which had so blessed me in one aspect of my spiritual life would equally bless me in other aspects of it. Hence, I began to read and study the Bible with a new avidity. But I soon found that I needed help, in order to know how to study. It was thus, the next summer, that I was led to attend the Conference of Believers, which was held at Niagara-on-the-Lake, Ontario, near Niagara Falls. This Conference greatly helped me. At the same time, it revealed to me my ignorance, and to a degree that was not a little discouraging. I needed, evidently, not only further help, but also, help of a more personal kind. Thus, the following winter, I asked the secretary of the Conference, Dr. William J. Erdman, to visit the village of Attica, in order to give there some Bible Readings, and to be my teacher while resident in our home. Dr. Erdman

accepted the invitation and became our guest. The inter-
course which followed began a sacred friendship, which lasted
until his death and which meant to me an ever increasing
spiritual blessing.

Dr. Erdman, in undertaking to teach me, took—as it then
seemed to me—a strange course. He began his expositions of
the Word, not in the New Testament, but in the Old; and he
chose as his subject of exposition the dream of Nebuchadnezzar,
as recorded in the second chapter of the book of Daniel. The
subject was certainly interesting, but, at first, it did not
appear to me to be altogether practical. My teacher, however,
proved wiser than most instructors would have been, for I
would add that that exposition led to the changing of the
whole current of my life. Before the Doctor had finished his
explanations, I was brought to see that the great objective
which God, in the present age, had set before Himself and
the church, was the coming of Christ, and that in that coming
the hope of both the church and the world was bound up.
This perception did more than give to me, as I believe, the
true key to the interpretation of the Scriptures; it led me to
perceive the relative worth of things, as between those which
were earthly and heavenly, temporal and eternal. And it was
thus that it came to pass, among various influences, that
God eventually constrained me to dedicate my life to foreign
missions. This I did, for one reason, that I might do all that
in me lay to hasten the accomplishment of those providential
events, the fulfillment of which would make possible the
coming of the King and His kingdom.

The experience which I had with Dr. Erdman directed me
into a careful study of the prophetic Scriptures, and for a
considerable time afterwards I found this part of the Word
the most interesting and helpful of all its various topics. The
time came, however, when I discovered that prophetic study
had become somewhat of a snare to me. I had reached the
point where my interest was centering in what I may call
the curiosities of the Scriptures, and where I was more
anxious to learn about the things which were new than to
put into practical use those which were old. This discovery
produced, though only for the time being, a reaction from

the study of prophecy. I now realized, whatever events were to take place in the days to come and however important these were, that there were also present days to be faced, with their pressing opportunities and obligations. Hence, it became my longing to know what sort of a Christian God would have me be, what kind of service He expected me to render, and what were the privileges in Christ which He had set before me. Such considerations as these led me into a new reading of the Old and New Testaments, but now, with a wider view and a more personal application. As a result of this experience, I began to study the great fundamental doctrines of the Christian faith; and, later, I came to the contemplation of such experimental themes as those of prayer, praise, consecration, sanctification, etc.

It was in this way that I finally undertook a close, and, what has turned out to be, a long study of the Scriptures concerning the subject of miraculous healing. This topic was almost thrust upon me, for the experience of my personal and family life demanded it, and besides, some close and esteemed friends earnestly urged it upon me. Thus it was, at different times, that I read and re-read the Scriptures with this one subject in mind, marking on the margin of my Bible every reference to it. As I write, there lies before me an analyzed Bible reading, which was worked out as a result of this course of study, and which has noted within it every important passage in the New Testament referring to God's healing of the body. And it is fitting that I should add that I shall never cease to be grateful to God that I was thus led to face this part of Scripture testimony. What prophecy did for me in one direction, this doctrine did in another. Among other things, it brought God nearer to me and myself nearer to God; and, above all, it impressed upon me the truth that the Christ in heaven has all power upon earth, and His present interest in the members of His body is as close and compassionate as it was when He was on earth amongst men. As for the general result of my study, it was a simple and blessed one. I argued thus: If Jesus were on earth and I needed Him for healing, I should go to Him for this even as others went to Him; as He is not on earth, I cannot go to Him in person; nevertheless,

I may reach Him by faith where He is in heaven, and, since He is not changed in character, I may expect Him to heal where there is need, even as He used to heal. At a later period and after further study of the Word, I was forced somewhat to modify my conclusions as expressed in the last clause of this statement. I am constrained to add, nevertheless, that the proposition as a whole seems to me as true today as it did when I first formulated it.

The conclusion concerning miraculous healing which I had now reached, brought me into an attitude of mind and heart where I desired to make practical application of my new-found privilege. As time went on, therefore, I looked more and more to God for health, and also, for healing when health had failed. And I would gladly and gratefully testify that God did not disappoint me. On the contrary, in many instances, He heard my prayers and gave gracious answers to my petitions. As a child, I had been sickly and weak; and, as a man, I was far from strong. But the Lord, in a new way, sustained me in the midst of a heavy and an increasingly arduous life-service; and, often He gave me to see His power in restoring myself and others from serious sickness.

It is not strange, in view of the above, that my faith in God as a strengthener and healer, as the years passed by, was both confirmed and increased. For the same reasons it is not strange that I now write in deep sympathy with those persons who hold the doctrine of miraculous healing. Yea, I confess that it is my present, deep conviction that Christ does strengthen and heal, and that He is more often ready to do the one and the other for those who put their trust in Him than most Christians realize. For this reason, it is my object in writing this book to do what I can to influence Christians to remember this almost forgotten truth, and to return to what, it seems to me, is the scriptural attitude in respect to it. It is my ardent hope, therefore, that my words may be used of God to induce not a few of His children to place an altogether new confidence in Christ as One who cares, not only for the soul, but also and as tenderly, for the body; for I am convinced that the man who sees to it, in all respects, that "the body" is "for the Lord," will make discovery, sooner or later, of the fact that "the Lord," in His turn, is most truly and blessedly "for the body." And I think that it will generally be admitted, in this world of suffering, that this is a consummation which is greatly to be desired.

But I must not end here. As I desire to be entirely frank from the beginning, I would state that I have an additional motive in writing this record and exposition. It seems to me that there is special need at the present time and that there will be increasing need as time goes on, for Christians to hold all truth in careful equipoise. Satan, in seeking to destroy the peace and usefulness of the children of God, has many methods of attack, and none is more effective than when he attempts to lead them into unbalanced and extravagant positions. This last is particularly true when he is able to approach them along the line of self-interest, where he may tempt them to take up with given theories because it is personally profitable to do so. The mere statement of such a possibility shows that there is a peculiar danger to the Christian in accepting and holding the doctrine of miraculous healing. That God will maintain him in health and strength, that He will immediately heal him if sick, is a prospect which appeals to any man, whether he be spiritual or otherwise. It is here that Christian Science and the Emmanuel Movement have found their place and power; and, I believe that it is here also, in part, that the doctrine of miraculous healing, especially as it has generally been taught, has made its appeal to the hearts and lives of the children of God. There appears on the very face of this question, therefore, a look of danger, to which every true disciple of Christ needs to give heed. Any doctrine may easily be distorted; but here is one which, in the nature of the case, may readily be thrown into large disproportion by one who holds it and enjoys its benefits. And this, it seems to me, many persons have done and are doing, and with serious consequences.

As to the seriousness of the matter, it is to be remembered that the occupying of any super-scriptural position will eventually lead one, if he is honest, into discouragement and despondency; for such a person will never be satisfied unless he fully and constantly attains to what he believes is his privilege in Christ, and, if he holds something to be a privilege which God has never provided as such, the non-attainment of it must necessarily produce reaction, with disastrous spiritual results. Such an experience will mean that the man of God will conclude, either that God for some reason has forsaken him, or that he himself in some particular has forsaken God, when as a matter of fact neither the one nor the other may be true. I have seen many such cases in connection with the doctrine of miraculous healing, some of which have been unspeakably sad, where, because of the holding of an unscriptural and unworkable theory, the saint, in spite of a complete life-consecration, was living in the darkness of despondency, amounting in some cases to despair. The only correction of such an experience, is to come down from the unwarranted scriptural position which has been assumed, to solid scriptural ground, and there to abide. Such a course may not make for a sense of peculiarity or for an extra reputation of sanctity; but it will certainly lead to heart-rest and a true testimony before God and man.

I am writing, therefore, with a desire to lead such Christians as may read these words and may need help to what, I trust, is a rational conception of the doctrine of miraculous healing. Having confidence that God has granted to me, both from Scripture and experience, some measure of understanding of this important subject, I would humbly seek to pass on whatever I know, in the hope that it may be for the comforting and strengthening of some of Christ's dear servants. May I assure my reader that I shall be in constant prayer as I write, in order that I may not lead others astray from the truth; and I fervently trust that the reader will be in a like spirit of prayer. I make no apology for the personal and familiar form in which I put my words. I choose this intentionally, because it best suits my purpose, and also, because I wish what I say to be not so much an argument, as what the title-page specifies, a personal testimony. Whether the testimony may rightfully be considered an argument, it will be for the reader to decide.

II

INDIVIDUALS HEALED

I HAVE said that when I had learned to look to God for strength and healing, He graciously gave me to see not a little of His power in this respect, both in my own life and in the lives of others. It may be helpful now for me to mention some of the experiences which illustrate this fact. And in doing this, it will be my attempt in writing, not to overstate any fact, but rather, if I err at all, to do so upon the side of understatement. I am specially concerned about this point, for obviously hyperbole has no place in such a subject as this, and to give way to it in any degree would be to open the door to error of a serious kind. Let me then speak as sanely as possible of certain experiences which I have had.

While I was still a young man and living at Attica, New York, the Lord led me out from my business life into that of an evangelist. It was thus that I came one winter to hold a series of meetings at a town named Albion, New York, which was situated not far from my home. From the first of those meetings, God graciously gave His marked blessing. The services were well attended, Christians were edified, and the unconverted were saved. In this way, the meetings went on for about ten days out of the two weeks which had been set for their continuance. But just then misfortune overtook me. Passing, one evening, from the heated room of the church into the wintry chill of the streets, I caught a heavy cold, which settled in my throat. The next evening in the service, my voice quite failed me, so that I could scarcely be heard, even by those who sat in the front seats. When I returned to my room that night, my throat was inflamed and sore, and I could not speak above a whisper. As things were, evidently, I could not possibly continue the services, and there was no time, either for medical treatment or for the restoration which might come from rest.

As I knelt in prayer that night, before retiring, I asked God if He would not heal me, in order that the meetings might go on to their conclusion, and particularly, in order that additional souls might be blessed and saved. In spite of prayer, it was some time before I got to sleep because of pain in my throat and difficulty in breathing. But, at last, I did so. I slept on then to what must have been the middle of the night. At that time, I awoke for a few minutes, and, in that brief period, I was suddenly conscious of the fact that my throat was entirely well. When I awoke in the morning, the momentary impression of the night was amply confirmed. Beside the faintest reminder of the fact that I had had a cold, my throat was entirely healed. The pain had ceased, the cough was gone, and I could speak as easily and distinctly as usual. The meetings went on through the remaining days, and an increasing measure of blessing was granted to the end. The cold from which I had suffered did not return.

In 1901, toward the close of the Boxer trouble in China, I was asked by Mr. Hoste, the General Director of the China Inland Mission, to proceed to Shanghai, in order to meet there Mr. Walter B. Sloan, of London, and to hold with him a series of meetings, in behalf of the missionaries, for the deepening of their spiritual life. I gladly accepted this invitation and had the joy, when I set forth, of having, as my companion for the journey, a member of our Toronto Council, Mr. J. D. Nasmith. Thus, we took our way across the American continent to San Francisco, and set sail, on a wintry day, from that port.

When we reached the ocean, outside of the "Golden Gate," we found that a heavy storm was on. Immediately, our steamer was being violently tossed to and fro in the sea. As a result, I had to seek my cabin and berth. Here I remained for two days, so sick that it seemed as if I could not live through the experience of it. Nor was I exaggerating the seriousness of my condition, for, besides the frightful nausea, my heart had failed, my feet and hands were like ice, my head was very dizzy and I had become so weak that the ship's doctor feared that I should not long survive. At last, lying there in my weakness, I asked myself certain questions.

First, What had been my object in setting forth for China? I answered myself, or rather, the Lord, that it had been to go out and remind our beloved missionaries of the joy of both doing and suffering the will of God. And then, Was I myself willing to do and suffer God's will at all times, and especially just then and there, as related to my present sickness? I found it more difficult to answer this question than the first one, for I knew not what the issue might mean to me. But finally, I looked upward to Him who sat upon the throne and said, "By Thy grace, Lord, I am willing to go to China or not; to go onward or downward; to live for Thee or die for Thee; whatever Thou shalt choose, to that will I say a glad Amen!" And then came a wonderful experience. Instantaneously, as soon as this prayer had arisen from my heart, the sickness left me. At once, the nausea ceased, my hands and feet became warm, and I felt a sense of strength which was delightful and for which I did not find it difficult to praise God. Immediately, though the steamer was still tossing in the storm, I got up and dressed. Later, I went on deck. And from that time on, until we reached Shanghai, I remained perfectly well.

At another time, I had the following experience in China, in connection with the Rev. J. Hudson Taylor. Having broken down with nervous prostration, I went to that country for change and rest, and also, to see the work of the Mission. But instead of being better on my arrival in Shanghai, I was worse; and, in spite of calling godly brethren together to pray for me and, according to the injunction in the Epistle of James, to anoint me with oil, there followed months of weakness, which kept me, for the most part, confined to my room, and generally to my couch or bed. This experience of trial was increased by finding that Mr. Taylor was even more seriously sick than I was, a condition of things which put a natural gloom over all of my days as they were lived out in the Mission compound. At last, however, the summer passed, and the cooler weather of the fall came on. By this time, both Mr. Taylor and I were somewhat better. This fact led to the suggestion being made that we, together with Mrs. Taylor, should take a houseboat and go up the Soo-chow

Creek, to the Soo-chow Hills. It was thus, one Saturday noon, that we set forth, and we were well on our way by that evening, when we anchored, not only for the night but also for the following Lord's Day.

As can be imagined, it was a pleasing experience to be away from the city and out in the country, and it was particularly so to Mrs. Taylor and myself, for Mr. Taylor had evidently left his many cares behind him and seemed as happy as a child. But the following Sunday morning I met with a great disappointment. As I arose, Mrs. Taylor informed me that Mr. Taylor had been taken ill in the night and was seriously sick. The old difficulty of heart-weakness, from which he had suffered so long and seriously and eventually died, had suddenly returned, and there seemed to be little life left in his body. When, later, I saw Mr. Taylor, my gravest fears were aroused, though I said little of this to Mrs. Taylor. And as the day went on, the situation became increasingly grave, for, manifestly, the dear sufferer was sinking lower and lower. Moreover, we were peculiarly helpless, even from a natural standpoint, for we could not do anything for Mr. Taylor, physicians being far away and ourselves having no remedies with us for heart-failure. At last, even brave, trustful Mrs. Taylor almost lost hope.

It was in this attitude of mind, feeling that God Himself must send help if the precious life was to be spared, that Mrs. Taylor came to me in my section of the boat, and asked if I would not unite with her in prayer for Mr. Taylor's healing. This, of course, I gladly consented to do. I said to my friend, at the same time, that I felt that God would have us begin with praise, to which suggestion she quickly agreed. I then read the last few Psalms, and, as I did so, emphasized their messages of thanksgiving. After this I prayed, beginning with praise. In doing this last, I thanked God for His many mercies, and then went on to thank Him for Mr. Taylor's sickness and his present serious condition, recognizing that perfect love was permitting all. After this, I asked our heavenly Father, if it might be His will, to raise up Mr. Taylor and to spare his valuable life. Mrs. Taylor followed with prayer, and she too began with praise.

Subsequent to this, we spent the time in that part of the boat where Mr. Taylor was lying. Never shall I forget his appearance. He was dressed in Chinese dress; his red and blue "wind cap" was pulled down over his head and shoulders; his hands were crossed over his body; his white beard covered his breast; his eyes were fast closed; his face was deathly pale; and his breath came and went in fitful gasps, which made us feel that each breath might be the last. There, we watched in silence, praising and praying. And while waiting thus, this blessed thing happened. Suddenly, Mr. Taylor's breath became easier, more steady, and more full. Then we noticed that the colour of his face and hands was improving. Finally, we saw that he had fallen asleep. And thus he lay, until the night came on. I heard no movements in the boat during the night, and the next morning I learned that the hours had passed quietly and peacefully. Quite early the following Monday morning, we started upon our way. In the afternoon we reached the Soo-chow Hills, and in the late afternoon, Mr. Taylor led us out over the same, walking without help and as if no serious sickness had been near him. It is not too much to say, that he seemed to us, as we watched him, like one who had been raised from the dead.

Some years since, one evening at Germantown, a Christian gentleman, Mr. S., called upon me to ask for my prayers. He looked, as he sat before me, the picture of despair, which did not seem strange when I heard the story which he related to me. The tale was as follows: The gentleman's daughter had been brought up with many advantages and had developed marked mental ability. She had prepared for a higher education, and later had been graduated from a leading college in Pennsylvania. She had, still later, gone to France in order to perfect herself in the French language, had then returned home, and had subsequently, for some years, pursued a brilliant career as a teacher in the college from which she had been graduated. Then, in the midst of her high success, she had suddenly become insane. As her insanity was not of a violent type, but more of the nature of imbecility, the parents had found it possible to keep their daughter in their home. At the same time, the strain of watching and caring for her was a most serious one; and the experience of seeing her, who had been so beautiful and bright, wholly blasted in mind and spirit was heart-breaking. Moreover, the physicians, though many had seen her, had failed to do her any good, and thus they had finally pronounced her incurable, so that now, after six years of sickness, the situation seemed an utterly hopeless one, except as God might be pleased to interpose and heal. My friend had come to me, therefore, to ask if I would not pray that healing might be granted.

I considered it, of course, a joy to unite in prayer with this sorely tried father, and, after some talk about the privilege of prayer, we knelt together before God and asked Him, since the physicians had failed, if it might not be His will to put forth His power and entirely restore her who was so sadly afflicted. Then and there we left the matter in the hands of a loving, heavenly Father. As to the result, I knew nothing for some nine months. After that space of time, Mr. S. reappeared at our home. One look at his face showed me that something joyful had occurred. Presently, he told me this tale:

The next day after he had been to see me, a friend of his daughter, living in Brooklyn, had asked her to visit in her home, and, in the hope that a change of location might prove helpful, the parents had consented to the arrangement and the father had taken the patient to her hostess. It turned out that this friend was a Christian Scientist, and it followed that she did all that she could, from the standpoint of her belief, to bring about a recovery. But no cure took place. Instead, the poor sufferer received a nervous shock from something which occurred in the home, which resulted in throwing her far back physically, and into a more serious mental condition than had before existed. At this, being concerned, the Christian Scientist took her to a neighbouring home and left her, and the ladies there telegraphed to the father to come and get his child.

It was thus, within three days, that the invalid was back at Germantown with her parents. There, in view of the increased mental derangement, the following hours brought new and more poignant sorrow. But one day, less than a week after we had prayed for the daughter, she suddenly put her hands to her head, looked up with a new light in her eyes, and, addressing her father, said, "Father, I don't know what has happened to me; a great cloud has been lifted from my mind, and all the darkness has gone!" From that time, the father had wished to come to see me, in order to tell me the good news of divine deliverance. But he had restrained himself from doing this, fearing that the healing might not prove permanent. Thus, the nine months had passed away. But thus also, at last, he had come to assure me that God had heard our petitions. His daughter, he said, was entirely and permanently recovered from her insanity, her physical strength had returned, she had resumed her normal study life, and all of her spiritual depression—she had thought that she had committed the unpardonable sin and was lost—had disappeared. It was for these reasons that my friend now desired me to unite with him in praise, as I had done before in prayer. My reader will understand that I considered it a great privilege to do this, in adoration of Christ, the mention of whose name before the Father had brought such a marvellous cure to pass. I made inquiries about the daughter some ten years after this. The father had died, but the brother reported that his sister was perfectly well.

A number of years ago, one day in the fall of the year, I was working in my office at Toronto, when the maid—who had come from the adjacent Mission Home—announced to me that a Mr. McC. was in the sitting-room of the Home and desired to see me. When I heard the visitor's name I jumped to my feet, wondering if it could be that my friend and Princeton classmate, James McC., was actually in our house and that I was to have the privilege of seeing him whom I had seen but once since we had parted at college, many years before. The maid, of course, could not inform me whether or not the visitor was my friend, and so I hastened from the office into the Home and thence down the stairs into the sitting-room, to find out if my surmise were true.

One glance showed me that my anticipation was a correct one, for there sat my old-time and ever dear friend. But I was shocked beyond expression at his appearance. Though the weather was mild, he had on a winter overcoat, which he had kept buttoned and was wearing even in the house with the collar turned up. His face was thin and haggard, his skin was sallow, and his eyes were dull and lifeless. He greeted me with a loving smile, and with still more loving words; yet he did not rise as I came in, but remained seated as he had been, in a sort of collapsed condition, as if he had been through a great sickness and was nearly at an end of his physical endurance. In college days, my friend had been well developed, strong and vigorous, and the reader will understand what my heart felt as I looked at him. Almost unconsciously, I began silently to pray for him, asking God what it all meant and what could be done. Then to my friend I said:

"James, where have you come from?"

Mr. McC. answered, "From the Georgian Bay district, where I have spent the summer."

At this I asked, "And where are you going?"

My friend replied, in a pathetically sad voice, "Ah, beloved, I am going home to die."

These words shocked me even more than his appearance had done, especially as his looks confirmed his words. But suddenly, in answer to my silent prayers, God gave me a great assurance and I spoke as I had never spoken before, as I have never spoken since, and as I should never again dare to speak except under a similar assurance. Looking at my friend I said, with almost prophetic positiveness,

"James, you are not going home to die; I will tell you what you are going to do: you are going upstairs to bed, you are going to let us care for you and you are going to get well."

"No," my friend replied, "that is not for me; and, as for my staying, I can't do this for I should give you too much trouble."

I answered, "There is not a person in this house to whom you can give trouble."

"But," he replied, "I have to have peculiar food."

"All right," I said, "we have a peculiar cook."

"No," he argued, "I have to prepare my own food."

"Very well," I also argued, "we have a room upstairs in which there is a gas stove, and where you can do all the cooking you desire." Then I continued: "Now, dear old chap, don't argue any more; just surrender and let me have my way."

And the dear fellow did surrender. In a short time I had him located in the room with the gas stove, and settled in bed, looking very worn and sick, but most grateful to have found a haven of welcome and rest. There, I had definite prayer with him that God would make him well; and there I left him for the evening and night.

At about ten o'clock the next morning, I knocked at Mr. McC.'s door and was bidden to come in, and in a tone of voice which I noticed was considerably stronger than the one I had heard the day before. Entering the room, I was surprised to find my friend was up and nearly dressed, and I was pleased to see that he looked refreshed and strengthened. Then, to my joy, he came across the room to me, put his hands upon my shoulders, looked with new brightness and courage into my face, and said, "Do you know, beloved, I don't believe I am going to die."

It was manifest that God had been pleased to answer prayer and, that physically, the turn of the tide had come. We sent for Dr. Sweetnam, our family physician, but he said that nothing medically could be done for him, and nothing was done. But from that hour, there was steady gain.

Mr. McC. had been sick with nervous prostration and resultant digestive trouble for some years, and though he had had the aid of physicians and the help of long summer outings, he had steadily grown worse, and this had continued until the time he had reached our home. But in the ten days he was with us, my friend added fifteen pounds to his weight, and after he left he continued to gain until he weighed as much as he had in college, namely, one hundred and eighty-five pounds. In addition, he was so strengthened in mind—he had not been able for a long time to think closely without much suffering—that he soon found it possible to resume his Christian service of Bible teaching, by voice and pen. In this last service, he has had to use much care not to overdo; but his activities for many years past now have been varied and great. In other words, when everything possible had been done to secure healing by natural processes, without result, God Himself, in answer to our united prayer, brought healing to pass. It was thus that he who had been slowly but surely dying and was then nigh unto death, was suddenly and permanently healed.

III

INDIVIDUALS NOT HEALED

IF I could leave my record where it stands, as given in the preceding chapter, it would not be possible for me to come to any but radical conclusions in respect to God's readiness to heal. But it is here where I must be careful not to exaggerate, and where I must be prepared to be honest, in the strictest sense of the word, whatever this may imply. It is my purpose, therefore, to add to the experiences of healing which have been mentioned some additional ones, where, though prayer was offered and faith was exercised, like healing was not given. And I would explain that the foregoing five cases of healing were chosen from the whole number which might have been given from my experience, not only because they were amongst the most notable, but also, because I desire to add to them five other cases of an almost exactly similar character. I choose this method of procedure for the reason that the parallelism thus established will simplify both the process of thought and the final deduction. If, say, in ten typical cases of sickness, certain conditions were fulfilled and the same result of healing was always obtained, then one would be justified in generalizing, and a single, uniform conclusion could be reached. But if, on the other hand, in ten typical cases, like conditions being fulfilled, five of these show one result, and five another, then a single generalization becomes impossible, and a new and different conclusion must be reached. The more particular intent of these observations will be understood as this testimony proceeds.

During the days of my evangelistic service, about a year after I had held the meetings previously referred to in Albion, New York, I was asked to return to that place and for the similar purpose of conducting evangelistic meetings. The services arranged for were to be held, as before, for two weeks, and there was anticipation, in view of the previous experience, of much blessing. But again it was mid-winter, and again, at evening, it was necessary to pass from the heated assembly room into the chilly air of the streets. Thus it was, after about a week of meetings, that I caught a heavy cold, which settled in my throat, inflaming it, producing hoarseness and soreness, and making it difficult for me to speak. Under such circumstances, especially with my past experience of healing in remembrance, it was a natural thing that I should go to God and ask for divine intervention. And this I did, with simple trust. But, upon this occasion, the expected healing did not take place. On the contrary, the hoarseness and soreness became aggravated. I then renewed my petitions before God, and with increased fervency. The result, however, was the same. My voice, by this time, was reduced to a low whisper, and I could not be heard in the meetings. It was thus that the services had to be brought to a conclusion before the set time had expired. As for my cold, it gradually passed away. But this was only after I had reached home, and the cure was brought to pass through the usual processes of rest and medical treatment.

In the year 1904, subsequent to the experience of healing from seasickness previously described, Mr. Hoste invited me to visit Shanghai, to take part there, with himself, Mr. Sloan and the members of the China Council, in the adjustment of certain difficulties which had arisen in the Mission. Dr. Howard Taylor was in America at the time, and the way was opened for him to visit China, so that I had the comfort of his companionship upon the journey. As at the previous time, the route across the continent to San Francisco was taken, and as before we sailed from that port. And as before, we ran into a storm, with all the consequences of a heavy sea and rolling steamer. In an hour's time, I was laid low, and, later, there came on severe seasickness, with accompanying heart-weakness. Finally, my condition became serious, and thus I gave myself, with what strength I had, to prayer for healing. But it was in vain. Then, in remembrance of my previous experience, being constrained to think that I had discovered a holy means of answered prayer, I committed myself, in the dedication of a new surrender, to God, for whatever His blessed will might choose for me. Once more, I told Him in all sincerity that I was willing to go to China or not; to go onward or downward; to live or die. The answer which God gave to me was unmistakable. He did not allow me to die; but He did allow me to be sick, and that without relief of any kind. For several days the physical conditions remained wholly unchanged, though they were not so serious as in the previous experience. At last, we drew near the Hawaiian Islands. There in the calm seas of that tropical clime, the ship ceased her tossings, and, as a result of this I gradually regained my usual health. This, happily, I retained until the end of the voyage at Shanghai.

Some time after God had so remarkably restored Mr. Hudson Taylor on the houseboat upon the Soo-chow Creek, Mr. and Mrs. Taylor journeyed from China to England, and on his way thither passed through Canada. In this manner they came to visit us in the Mission Home at Toronto. Mr. Taylor, when he reached us, was in poor health, and his condition, while remaining with us, grew worse. He was suffering, at the time, from a nervous trouble, which at last so affected the stomach that little food could be retained, or even taken. This meant that our brother's strength steadily declined; and thus the time came when he was so weak that he was confined to his room and to his bed or couch. Later, his old physical enemy, heart-weakness, set in, and, thereafter, his state was a serious one.

Mr. Taylor, up to this time, had been acting as his own physician; but his condition was now so grave that he consented to our calling the Mission doctor, that able practitioner and devoted man of God, Dr. Sweetnam. But, somehow, even Dr. Sweetnam's skill did not avail. As time went on, therefore, there was no change for the better. On the contrary our dear friend continued to fail. The many occupants of the Mission Home had been praying earnestly through the days which had passed. Now that things had reached a crisis, prayer was not only earnest, but also, importunate. There was private prayer, and united prayer; and through all, it was a strong crying unto God for deliverance. In spite of prayer and faith, however, the longed-for answer of healing was not granted. At last, a sense of helplessness took possession of us, for we knew not what to conclude. But just then, Mr. Taylor recalled a remedy which he had not thought of for a number of years, but which he had used in a former sickness with success. Dr. Sweetnam favoured its trial; and the medicine was obtained and taken. Immediately, there was a change for the better, and from that time on, there was steady improvement. Finally, a full recovery took place. Our beloved friend was able to resume his work, holding meetings, having interviews, etc., as usual. He afterwards went to England, where he passed through a heavy ordeal of ministry. Eventually, he returned to China to resume there his usual strenuous service. But this time it is to be noted, Mr. Taylor's recovery was through the use of medicine and not by the direct interposition of God.

Some years ago the Mission in America sent to China for service there a devoted young lady, a Miss De L., concerning whom we had many hopes. For a few years these hopes were amply realized, the blessing of God resting upon our friend in every particular. But then, sad news reached us. We were informed that insanity was developing, and, probably, that the young lady would have to be sent home. Later, she was brought from her station to Shanghai, where she was tenderly cared for during some weeks. But at this place her malady so increased that, escaping from her nurse one day, she sought death by throwing herself into the river, from which the police rescued her. There was much special prayer for her after this, but no change for the better occurred, and hence, as soon as proper escort had been provided, she was sent home to Canada. It was thus that she came into the Mission Home at Toronto, from whence she had gone out. Here, everything was done for her which love could suggest. Miss De L. had now repeatedly shown signs of a desire to destroy herself, so that constant companionship and watchfulness had to be provided for her. In addition, she was given, as had been the case in China, the help of constant, believing prayer. Medical aid in the case had proved valueless, and, for this reason, the petitions which were breathed were for God's direct and immediate healing. But days and weeks passed by without the desired answer being received.

It was at this time that I reached Toronto from Philadelphia, upon one of my periodical visits, and it was thus that I came into personal contact with the serious conditions which had developed. Our friend, more than ever, was bent upon committing suicide, that she might, as she told me, rise from the dead and so convince the world of God's infinite power. Hence, we went anew to God in prayer, crying out to Him for speedy healing. Healing, however, was not granted. I postponed action still longer, in hope that our gracious Father might send us His help. But the help for which we sought was not given to us. It was thus, at last, that I was forced to commit our friend to the Toronto Insane Asylum, where she could more easily be cared for, and where, particularly, she would be protected from self-destruction. Meanwhile, prayer was not remitted. Daily, the sufferer was remembered before God, and that by an ever widening circle of sympathizing friends.

To our joy, at last, in spite of the fact that the Asylum physician had told us that there never would be a recovery, prayer was markedly answered, for there was decided improvement. This continued till the decision was reached that Miss De L. might leave the Asylum and go to her home. Soon, thereafter, she left us for Boston. We got rather out of touch with her from that time on, though we occasionally heard about her, and we did not cease to pray for her. In this manner, nearly two years passed by. After this time, all the past was suddenly and startlingly brought before us. A paragraph in a newspaper told us that our poor friend had thrown herself into the bay near the city, that she had been rescued and taken to a hospital, but that she was critically ill and likely to die. We afterwards heard that she had recovered. But she was never fully healed, for a few years later she suddenly threw herself before a train and was instantly killed. This, then, is apparent: In the case of insanity previously mentioned, a single prayer was offered, and, though that case was a much more serious one than this, healing was almost immediately given; in this case, prayer was offered for many years, and by saints who seldom knew what it was to have prayer remain unanswered; but full healing was never given. In other words, the results in the two cases, though believing prayer was offered in each, were of a different and opposite kind.

Some years ago, Dr. P. was holding a series of meetings in the home of Miss Huston, at Germantown, Philadelphia. While thus engaged, he became afflicted with a malady which caused him so much physical pain that he was hardly able to continue the services which he had undertaken. To those who were attending the meetings and were aware of what was transpiring, the picture of God's suffering child was a pathetic one, especially to some of us who had known the Doctor for many years and had never before seen him in any but the best physical condition. It was reckoned a privilege by a few of us, therefore, to have him ask us to meet with him on a given afternoon that we might unite with him in prayer for divine help and deliverance.

The gathering took place at the home of Dr. W. J. Erdman, and besides Dr. P. there were present Dr. Erdman, Dr. Munhall, Pastor Stearns and myself. At the beginning of our prayer service, Dr. P. told us how the disease from which he was suffering had come upon him, apparently as a result of the activities of his Christian service which had involved much travelling and considerable exposure, and how he had prayerfully sought the help of physicians, but without avail. He then declared, since the physicians seemed powerless to help him, that he was convinced that only God could give him healing, and hence, he said that he craved our help before Him as we should ask, with one mind and heart, for a speedy and complete cure. He finally explained that much seemed to depend upon our obtaining an answer from God, because he had received important invitations for service at home and in England which he could not accept unless he should be healed, and also, because he was contemplating a tour around the world, which he hoped would mean much for foreign missions, but which could not possibly be taken unless he should have deliverance from suffering.

All of us who listened to Dr. P. as he spoke were deeply

impressed by the humility and trustfulness of his spirit, and also by the fact that he was seeking healing, not for his own comfort—though there was need of this—but for the glory of God and for the exaltation of the name of Christ. As our friend had asked to be anointed with oil, Dr. Erdman performed this rite. We then gave ourselves to prayer in his behalf with much readiness of mind; and we continued in this exercise for about two hours, feeling, on rising from our knees, that the Holy Spirit had indeed been in our midst and that we had been permitted through Him to have special access to the throne of grace. However, none of us had real assurance that Dr. P. would be healed. As for myself, I felt, first on that afternoon and then increasingly as I continued to pray, that God had appointed our brother to suffering, that he might bear witness, as he had never had opportunity in the past, to the sustaining grace and power of God.

The foregoing thought was so much in my mind that, a few days after the Doctor went back to his home, I took the liberty of writing to him, asking him not to be discouraged if God did not answer our prayers as we had offered them, and expressing the thought that it was possible that our all-wise and all-loving Father was going to ask a great thing of him, namely, to show forth Christ's life of trust and patience even in the furnace fire of affliction. Dr. P. thanked me for my letter; but, in writing to Dr. Erdman, he was able to give us the good news that, while he was not fully healed, he was so much better that he was largely freed from pain and was able to go on with his usual service. A little later, I was advised that the journey around the world had been decided upon.

Some time after this I had an invitation to attend and take part in a dinner which was to be given to Dr. P. and which was to be in the nature of a farewell to him. I was not able to accept of this invitation; and I will confess that I was relieved when I saw that this was the fact, for I could not help fearing what so long and arduous a journey might mean to one so advanced in years and so feeble in body, and hence that I should find myself somewhat out of sympathy with the purpose of the banquet. I mention this last in order to give

myself the opportunity to add that my prayers for Dr. P.,
as he set out upon his world tour, were increased, both in
frequency and intensity. Happily for me, it became possible
to make prayer intelligent, for his son kindly sent me copies
of his father's and sister's letters, describing the different
stages of the outward journey. Through these letters, the news
finally reached me that Dr. P. had broken down in Japan,
and more seriously in Korea, and, then again, that he was
returning home. He safely reached San Francisco and Los
Angeles, though in a weakened physical condition and in a
state of much suffering. At the latter place, I learned later,
our dear friend felt, once more, that God only could give
him relief from his sickness and pain, and he did that which
he had done before, namely, sent for godly men to anoint
him with oil and to pray with and for him.

After the foregoing, Dr. P. was somewhat better, and thus,
his relatives were able to bring him across the continent to
his home. There he waited the will of the Lord, while hundreds
of saints in various parts of the world who knew his need,
pleaded with God for his recovery. But the sufferer's strength
gradually and steadily declined. However, the thing for which
I had hoped came to pass. In spite of the fact that many
natural causes were against such a result, Dr. P. having
always lived a superabundantly active life and being naturally impatient of any restraint upon his activities, God's grace
triumphed and that supremely. Our beloved friend did not
once murmur, but, on the contrary, gave himself patiently
and even praisefully to the accepting of the will of God.
His sick room became thus a Bethel, and the severest testing
of his life was turned into the greatest victory which that
life had ever won for the Lord. At last, however, the pilgrim
journey ended, and the pilgrim saint fell asleep in Christ,
with the restfulness and trustfulness of a little child. The
last words upon the lips which had so long and blessedly
witnessed for the truth were those from the Epistle to the
Hebrews, "That we might be partakers of his holiness."
Nevertheless, it is the fact that in Mr. McC.'s case there was
healing, and in the similar case of Dr. P. there was not.

IV

VARIOUS OBSERVATIONS

IT will be observed that I have described in the last two chapters ten separate cases of sickness, with the details of which I am personally familiar. Also, it will be observed that God in answer to prayer, in the first five of these, gave direct and immediate healing, and in the last five, though prayer was offered, did not give such healing, but healed otherwise or did not heal at all. In addition, it will be observed that I have chosen and arranged the ten cases in such a manner as to establish a parallelism between them, each corresponding set having reference, for the most part, to similar conditions in respect to the persons who were sick, the kind of sickness which prevailed, and the person, or persons, who prayed for healing.

In view of this citation and combination, it is now possible to consider the whole number of the cases in order to attempt to gather from them warrantable conclusions. It must be remembered, however, that any deductions which may thus be made cannot be considered as, in themselves, final. Whatever conclusions may be reached must be submitted to the test of the Word of God, and only such deductions may stand as are found to be in correspondence with the Word. Thus two processes of reasoning will be brought into view. The first process may be regarded as a scientific one, having its real value; the second process will be recognized as a spiritual one, having a supreme value. At the same time, if the finding from the one process confirms that obtained from the other, and if the two are discovered to be in agreement, it may rationally be concluded that the truth, being witnessed to both by Scripture and experience, has been established and may rightfully affect both opinion and practice. The present chapter will be taken up, therefore, with the consideration of the ten cases which have been described, and with the attempt to

33

discover what the facts and principles are which they contain. I shall take the liberty, in proceeding, in view of my familiarity with the details of the cases, to state certain important features of them, which were not mentioned in the descriptions given. Also, for the sake of clearness, I shall put my conclusions in the form of a series of propositions.

It is to be noted, in all of the ten cases mentioned, that the use of means, as represented by physicians, nurses and medicines, was not rejected, either before, during, or after the experience of the sicknesses described. This signifies that God did not condition His acts of healing, in the five cases where He gave direct healing, upon the persons concerned assuming the attitude that the use of means was wrong and was inconsistent with full trust in God. On the contrary, it signifies that God granted direct healing even when means were regarded as allowable, and that He continued to grant such healings, in additional cases, in answer to the prayers of those who used such means.

It is to be noted in all of the ten cases mentioned, with two exceptions, that the individuals concerned did not send for the elders of the church in order that the sick person might be anointed with oil, and yet that God, in five cases, granted direct healing in answer to the prayers offered. It is to be noted also, in the two cases where anointing took place, that God did not answer prayer by direct healing. It is not meant to imply by these statements that the persons who had to do with the cases of sickness and did not have recourse to anointing disbelieved in taking the course described in the fifth chapter of the Epistle of James; nor is it meant to imply, prayer not having been answered in the two cases where anointing with oil took place, that the persons concerned concluded that anointing had been a mistake. The intention is simply to point out the fact that the conditions were as described. The conclusion, therefore, is rightfully reached that God, in the cases where direct healing was given, did not require that the injunction in the Epistle of James should be complied with, but, on the contrary, was pleased to heal apart from the fulfillment of that injunction. And the further conclusion is rightfully reached, that God, in the cases where anointing was practised, did not consider the obedience which led to the use of oil, even though believing prayer accompanied it, a sufficient reason why healing should in these cases be given.

It is to be noted, in all of the ten cases, that the attitude of those who prayed was not that of claiming healing, as if a universal right had been established by the atoning work of Christ, but rather that of seeking God's will in the given case, and of saying continually, "Thy will be done," until that will was made known. It also is to be observed, that this was the experience in all of the five cases where direct healing was granted as truly as it was in the five cases where healing was not granted.

It is to be noted in all of the five cases where direct healing was given that there were certain facts which gave them a peculiar character. In some cases, there was not time or opportunity to make use of the natural means of healing, if the Christian service which the individual had undertaken was to be continued and fulfilled. In other cases, means had been used and these had failed, so that there was no possibility of healing taking place unless God should bring this to pass in an unusual manner. And lastly, some special spiritual end was manifestly in view as a result of the healing given, such as the showing forth of Christ's power in a peculiarly striking and public way, or the raising up of an individual whose life was of importance in the fulfillment of God's purposes upon the earth.

It is to be noted that the conditions of prayer in the five cases of direct healing were not uniform, but dissimilar. In some cases, one prayed. In other cases, two united in prayer. In still other cases, many persons, sometimes widely separated, were agreed together in the prayer which was offered. Again, in some cases, prayer was offered but once. In other cases prayer was offered many times and through long periods of time. In addition, persons who prayed for healing were heard and answered who had never before had such an experience. And, still in addition, persons who had liberty in asking for healing at one time, did not obtain such liberty at another time; and also, after such liberty, in a given case, had passed away, it was, in some other case, fully restored. It may be added that the only common experience in the prayers for healing which were offered is found in the fact that they were addressed to the Father in the name of Christ, and that they were designed to be for the glory of God and the good of the individual for whom prayer was offered. But it is to be remembered that this last was as truly the fact in the cases where direct healing was not granted as in the cases where it was.

It is to be noted that the faith exercised was not generally of the kind where positive assurance of obtaining the thing asked for accompanied the prayer. There was assurance, so far as is known, in all of the ten cases; but this had reference to the power, love, and wisdom of God rather than to the fact that healing would take place. The general attitude of those who prayed, and hence, of those who exercised faith, was this: they believed that God could heal; that He would heal if it was for His glory and for the good of the person who was sick; and finally, that He could be trusted implicitly to do what was right and best. Thus, those who prayed left the issue of their prayers with the heavenly Father in child-like confidence, repeating the prayer for healing until His will was known, and accepting the answer when it came, whatever it was, with submissive and trustful praise. It is to be observed also, that this submission of faith was as true in the five cases where direct healing was given as in the five cases where it was not given.

It is to be noted, so far as the facts are known, that the nature of the faith exercised by those who prayed for healing did not differ as between the five cases where direct healing was given and the five cases where such healing was not given. Hence, it cannot be inferred, where direct healing was not given, that the persons praying did not believe, or, at least, did not believe sufficiently to have the prayers for healing answered. As a matter of fact, just the opposite of what might naturally have been expected in such respects sometimes took place. In the experiences which I had of praying for healing, with the one exception of my experience with Mr. McC., I am positive that I had no more consciousness that I was trusting God when prayer for direct healing was answered than I had when such prayer was not answered. Indeed, I am bound to say that I was sometimes more conscious of a confidence in God that He would heal when He did not heal than when He did. The natural explanation of this last is this: that God's answering prayer for healing, on a given occasion, strengthened my faith and thus encouraged me to believe more ardently, on a subsequent occasion, though the result in the second case turned out to be just the opposite of what it had been in the first one. This was the fact when I prayed the second time for the healing of my throat; when I prayed the second time for healing from seasickness, and when I prayed the second time for the healing of Mr. Taylor. It seems correct to conclude, therefore, that the putting forth of God's power to heal, while in answer to the prayer of faith, did not depend upon a peculiar quantity of faith, or even upon a peculiar quality of faith, but rather upon the fulfilling of other scriptural and spiritual conditions.

It is to be noted, in the cases where direct healing was delayed and in the five cases where it was not granted, that special spiritual blessings were given to the persons who were permitted to be sick, and that most of the persons, if not all of them, were finally constrained to testify that they believed that the sickness had proved to be even better than health could have been. Mr. McC. has affirmed that the things which did most to separate him from the world to God and give him power to testify of the exalted and glorified Christ was the valley-deep experience through which he passed in the months of his weakness and suffering. Mr. Taylor once told me that his greatest spiritual blessings had come to him in connection with his various sicknesses; and later he made to me the remarkable statement that all of the most important advance movements which had taken place in connection with the China Inland Mission, including its inception, had come as a direct result of some physical breakdown through which he had been called upon to pass. And, if I may be permitted to refer to my own experience in this connection, I would witness to the fact, that the deepest, the most precious, and the most abiding spiritual lessons which God has been pleased to teach me were learned in consequence of and during my various experiences of sickness. This last is particularly true in respect to the prayer-life, the praise-life, the life of dependence upon God, and the life which chooses to live, not for the seen, but for the unseen, not for the temporal but for the eternal. All of this has been so blessedly true in my own experience, that I am tempted to agree with the man who said: "Health is the best thing in the world—except sickness!" Indeed, knowing what God has done for me through physical weakness, and being persuaded that certain blessings could never have been given to me in any other way than through such an experience, I feel that it would have been nothing short of a calamity to have missed the physical suffering through which I have passed.

It is to be noted, in all of the five cases where direct healing was given, that the process of healing was not a gradual one, but was instantaneous; and also, so far as the disease which was healed is concerned, that it was accomplished once for all. It is not meant by this that God always answered prayer as soon as it was offered. This was the case in some instances. But in some others, prayer was offered for a long time before deliverance was given. It remains a fact, however, in each of the five cases where direct healing was granted, that when the healing came it was immediate and lasting. In other words, from the moment of healing, prayer was turned into praise, and the petitions which had been offered did not have to be repeated.

It is to be noted, in all of the five cases where prayer for direct healing was answered, that, while the disease healed did not recur, other minor ailments, or even more serious diseases, were experienced, which needed to be faced and dealt with as previous sicknesses had been. I was healed of my cold; but I had many subsequent colds. I was healed of my seasickness; but since then I have frequently been seasick. Mr. McC. was lifted from the place of death; but he has had to take special care of his body and has found that there is a decided physical limitation upon him. Mr. Taylor was frequently recovered by God from severe sicknesses and his life was long lengthened out in spite of a weak heart; but other sicknesses came upon him, and at last it was through heart-failure that his earthly life came to an end.

It is finally to be noted, in all of the ten cases, while the granting of direct healing was evidently connected with holiness of life on the part of the person healed or on the part of the person or persons praying, that such holiness was not, in itself, a sufficient cause of healing. With the exception of the persons who were insane, there was special fellowship with God being enjoyed; and it is possible, even in the cases excepted, that this was the fact, as far as the physical conditions permitted. Admitting then, that a real measure of holiness of life was existing in all of the cases, it is to be observed that the results in the two sets of cases were different and opposite, the persons in the first five cases being healed, and the persons in the second five cases not being healed. It may be stated as a fact therefore, as far as the existing conditions are known, that those persons who were not healed were as much in fellowship with God when prayer was not answered as at other times or in other cases when it was; and also, that the persons who offered prayer for the person sick were as much in fellowship with God when their prayers were not answered as, at previous or subsequent times, when they were. Speaking for myself, I am positive that I have sometimes met with God's refusal to heal when I have been most in fellowship with Him. And taking Mr. Taylor as an illustration of one who maintained, by the Spirit, a pre-eminently close fellowship with God, I can affirm, as a result of personal observation and of the testimony of the one who knew him best, namely, Mrs. Taylor, that the times of his physical weakness were not times of his spiritual declension, but, contrariwise, they were commonly the times of his closest communion with Christ.

I venture to give here, in closing this chapter, and in confirmation of the foregoing statement, a story which relates to almost the last physical sickness of Mr. Taylor, which finally ended with his death. It was at the time when Mr. Taylor was living, as an invalid, at Davos, Switzerland, and when the Boxer trouble was raging in China. As the news of that calamity was received by cables and letters, Mr. Taylor's heart, which was always deeply and tenderly concerned for his missionaries, suffered keenly. He said, except to God, very little; but his wife and others saw that the shocking news of suffering and death was vitally affecting the already weakened body and that his strength was failing fast. From that time on most of the adverse news had to be kept from him. This, however, did not arrest the physical decline. At last, the beloved sufferer was so far spent that about all he could do was to lie on a sofa in his sitting room, where he was daily placed for change and rest, and patiently wait the issue, whatever it might be. While lying thus one day, he spoke to his wife as follows: "I cannot read; I cannot pray; I can scarcely think, but," he added with a smile, "I can trust!" And these memorable words characterized, not only Mr. Taylor's life in general, but also and particularly, all of those final years wherein weakness was his constant portion. It was such an one as this whom God permitted, in the very consummation of his holy living and believing, to be laid aside in great weakness and in frequent pain, until, at last, in far away China, overfatigue was added to debility, and he quietly and peacefully fell asleep in Christ.

V

TWO WITNESSES

IN the long history of the church, subsequent to the apostolic days, there have been many saints who have held and taught physical healing by the alone power of God. Justin Martyr, Irenaeus, Tertullian, Origen and Clement proclaimed the fact that the age of miracles had not passed, and that God was still prepared to heal the bodies of sick saints. Augustine, Luther, Melanchthon, Baxter, Bengel, Edward Irving, Bushnell, Grotius, Lavater, Hugh McNeil and Thomas Boys favoured in teaching and practice the doctrine of healing by prayer and faith. Dorothea Trudel, Pastor Blumhardt, Pastor Otto Stockmayer, Pastor Rein and Dr. Cullis are individual Christians whose ministry is associated, by common consent and on the basis of well-authenticated facts, with the divine gift and power of physical healing. And there have been companies of Christians, such as the Moravians and early English Methodists, which have encouraged their members to accept miraculous physical healing as a divinely established truth, and, it may be admitted, "with signs following."[1]

Among those persons whose names are closely associated with the doctrine of healing apart from physical means, two Americans stand out in particular conspicuousness. These are the late Dr. A. J. Gordon, of Boston, Massachusetts, and the late Dr. A. B. Simpson, of New York City. There are various reasons for the prominence of these two teachers in this field of thought: First, they were unusually godly men; second, they were uncommonly sane men; and third, they formulated their convictions, in a logical and convincing manner, in two books, which were widely circulated and largely accepted as representing God's truth. Dr. Gordon's book bore the title of

[1] See *The Ministry of Healing*, published by Howard Gannett, Tremont Temple, Boston, Massachusetts.

The Ministry of Healing; and Dr. Simpson's that of *The Gospel of Healing*. The former volume has more or less ceased to be bought and read. But the latter one, having the endorsement of the Christian and Missionary Alliance, remains in the market and has still a wide circulation. These two publications have come to be considered, both in North America and in countries beyond the Atlantic, as standard works upon the subject of miraculous healing; and it is universally admitted that their authors, because of their holy lives, forceful teaching and, for the most part, consistent practising in the matter of healing, are to be regarded as those whose testimony deserves most careful consideration. It is with this last thought in mind that I purpose now to quote from Dr. Gordon and Dr. Simpson.

Dr. Gordon, in *The Ministry of Healing*, writes as follows:

"In the atonement of Christ there seems to be a foundation laid for faith in bodily healing. Seems, we say, for the passage to which we refer is so profound and unsearchable in its meaning that one would be very careful not to speak dogmatically in regard to it. But it is at least a deep and suggestive truth that we have Christ set before us as the sickness-bearer as well as the sin-bearer of his people. In the gospel it is written, 'And he cast out the spirits with his word and healed all that were sick, that it might be fulfilled which was spoken by Esaias the prophet saying, Himself took our infirmities and bare our sicknesses' (Matt. 8:17). Something more than sympathetic fellowship with our sufferings is evidently referred to here. The yoke of his cross by which he lifted our iniquities took hold also of our diseases; so that it is in some sense true that as God 'made him to be sin for us who knew no sin,' so he made him to be sick for us who knew no sickness. He who entered into mysterious sympathy with our pain which is the fruit of sin, also put himself underneath our pain which is the penalty of sin. In other words the passage seems to teach that Christ endured vicariously our diseases as well as our iniquities.

"If now it be true that our Redeemer and substitute bore our sicknesses, it would be natural to reason at once that he bore them that we might not bear them. And this inference is especially strengthened from the fact, that when the Lord Jesus removed the burden of disease from 'all that were sick,' we are told that it was done 'that the scripture might be fulfilled, Himself took our infirmities and bare our sicknesses.' Let us remember what our theology is in regard to atonement for sin. 'Christ bore your sins, that you might be delivered from them,' we say to the penitent. Not sympathy—a suffering with, but substitution—a suffering for, is our doctrine of the cross; and therefore we urge the transgressor to accept the Lord Jesus as his sin-bearer, that he may himself no longer have to bear the pains and penalties of his disobedience. But should we shrink utterly from reasoning thus concerning Christ as our pain-bearer? We do so argue to some extent at least. For we hold that in its ultimate consequences the atonement affects the body as well as the soul of man. Sanctification is the consummation of Christ's redemptive work for the soul; and the resurrection is the consummation of his redemptive work for the body. And these meet and are fulfilled at the coming and kingdom of Christ.

"The ministry of the apostles, under the guidance of the Comforter, is the exact facsimile of the Master's. Preaching the kingdom and healing the sick; redemption for the soul and deliverance for the body—these are its great offices and announcements. Certain great promises of the gospel have this double reference to pardon and cure. The commission for the world's evangelization bids its messengers stretch out their hands to the sinner with the message, 'He that believeth shall be saved,' and to 'lay hands on the sick and they shall recover.' The promise by James, concerning the prayer of faith, is that it 'shall save the sick, and if he have committed sins they shall be forgiven him.' Thus this twofold ministry of remission of sins and remission of sickness extends through the days of Christ and that of the apostles.

"This promise given in Mark emerges in performance in the Acts of the Apostles. But it is significant and to be carefully observed, that the miraculous gifts are not found exclusively in the hands of the apostles. Stephen and Philip and Barnabas exercised them. These did not belong to the twelve, to that special and separated body of disciples with whom it has been said, that the gifts were intended to remain. It was not Stephen an apostle, but 'Stephen a man full of faith and of the Holy Ghost,' 'Stephen full of faith and power' that 'did great wonders and miracles among the people' (Acts 6:5, 8). We in these days cannot be apostles: but we are commanded to be 'filled with the Spirit,' and therefore are at least required and enjoined to have

Stephen's qualifications. According to the teaching in Corinthians it is as members of Christ's body and partakers of His Spirit, that we receive these truths."

Dr. Simpson, in *The Gospel of Healing*, writes as follows:

"Man has a twofold nature. He is both a material and a spiritual being. And both natures have been equally affected by the fall. His body is exposed to disease; his soul is corrupted by sin. How blessed, therefore, to find that the complete scheme of redemption includes both natures, and provides for the restoration of physical as well as the renovation of spiritual life! The Redeemer appears among men with His hands stretched out to our misery and need, offering both salvation and healing. He offers Himself to us as a Saviour to the uttermost; His indwelling Spirit the life of our spirit; His resurrection body the life of our mortal flesh.

"The earliest promise of healing is in Ex. 15:25, 26: 'There he made for them a statute and an ordinance, and there he proved them, and said, If thou wilt diligently hearken to the voice of the Lord thy God, and wilt do that which is right in his sight, and wilt give ear to his commandments, and keep all his statutes, I will put none of these diseases upon thee, which I have brought upon the Egyptians: for I am the Lord thy God which healeth thee.' The place of this promise is most marked. It is at the very outset of their journey, like Christ's healing of disease at the opening of His ministry.

"It comes immediately after the passage of the Red Sea. And we know that this event was distinctly typical of our redemption, and that the journey of the Israelites in the wilderness is typical of our pilgrimage: 'These things happened unto them for ensamples; and are written for our admonition, upon whom the ends of the world are come' (1 Cor. 10:11). This promise, therefore, becomes ours, as the redeemed people of God. And God meets us at the very threshold of our pilgrimage with the covenant of healing, declaring that, as we walk in holy and loving obedience, we shall be kept from sickness, which belongs to the old life of bondage we have left behind us forever. Sickness belongs to the Egyptians, not to the people of God. And only as we return spiritually to Egypt, do we return to its malarias and perils. Nay, this is not only a promise; it is 'a statute and an ordinance.' And so, corresponding to this ancient statute, the Lord Jesus has left for us in Jas. 5:14 a distinct ordinance of healing in His name as sacred and binding as any of the ordinances of the gospel.

"Isa. 53:4, 5: 'Surely he hath borne our griefs, and carried our sorrows . . . and with his stripes we are healed.'

"This is the great evangelical vision, the gospel in the Old Testament, the very mirror of the coming Redeemer. And here in the front of it, prefaced by a great Amen—the only 'surely' in the chapter—is the promise of healing, the very strongest possible statement of complete redemption from pain and sickness by His life and death, and the very words which the Evangelist afterwards quotes, under the inspired guidance of the Holy Ghost (Matt. 8:17) as the explanation of His universal works of healing.

"The translation in our English version does very imperfect justice to the force of the original. The translation in Matt. 8:17 is much better: 'Himself took our infirmities, and bare our sicknesses.' The literal translation would be: 'Surely he hath borne away our sicknesses, and carried away our pains.'

"Any person who will refer to such a familiar commentary as that of Albert Barnes on Isaiah, or any other Hebrew authority, will see that the two words here used denote respectively sickness and pain, and that the words for 'bear' and 'carry' denote not mere sympathy, but actual substitution and the removal utterly of the thing borne.

"Therefore, as He has borne our sins, Jesus Christ has also borne away and carried off our sicknesses; yes, and even our pains, so that abiding in Him, we may be fully delivered from both sickness and pain. Thus 'by his stripes we are healed.' Blessed and glorious gospel! Blessed and glorious Burden-Bearer!

"It would take entirely too long to examine in detail the countless records of His healing power and grace, or tell how He cured the leper, the lame, the blind, the palsied, the impotent, the fever-stricken, all 'that had need of healing'; how He linked sickness so often with sin, and forgave before He spake the restoring word; how He required their own personal touch of appropriating faith, and bade them take the healing by rising up and carrying their bed; how His healing went far beyond His own immediate presence, and reached and saved the centurion's servant and the nobleman's son, and how often He reproved the least question of His willingness to help, and threw the responsibility of man's suffering on his own unbelief.

"These and many more such lessons crowd every page of the

Master's life, and still reveal to us the secret of claiming His healing power. And what right any one can claim to explain away these miracles as mere types of spiritual healing and blessing, and not as specimens of what He still is ready to do for all who trust Him, is quite inexplicable. Such was Jesus of Nazareth.

"Jas. 5:14: 'Is any sick among you? let him call for the elders of the church; and let them pray over him, anointing him with oil in the name of the Lord: and the prayer of faith shall save the sick, and the Lord shall raise him up; and if he have committed sins, they shall be forgiven him.'

"Now, let us notice first who gives this commission. It is James who had authority to say, in summing up the decrees of the Council at Jerusalem (Acts 15:19): 'My sentence is,'—the man who is named first by Paul himself among the pillars of the church (Gal. 2:9).

"Again, observe to whom this power is committed. Not the apostles, who are now passing away, not men and women of rare gifts and difficult of access, but the elders, the men most likely to be within reach of every sufferer, the men who are to continue till the end of the age.

"Again, notice the time at which this commission is given. Not at the beginning, but at the close of the apostolic age; nor for that generation, but for the one that was just rising, and all the succeeding ages. For, indeed, these New Testament Epistles were not widely circulated in their own age, but were mainly designed 'for our admonition upon whom the ends of the world are come.'

"Again, observe the nature of the ordinance enjoined—'the prayer of faith,' and the 'anointing with oil in the name of the Lord.' Now, this was manifestly not a medical anointing, for it was not to be applied by a physician, but by an elder, and must, naturally, be the same anointing of which we read (Mark 6:13 and elsewhere), in connection with the healing of disease by the apostles themselves. Any other interpretation would be strained and contrary to the obvious meaning of the custom, as our Lord and His apostles observed it. In the absence of any explanation here to the contrary, we are bound to believe that it was the same—a symbolical religious ordinance expressive of the power of the Holy Ghost, whose peculiar emblem is oil. The Greek Church still retains the ordinance. The Romish apostasy has changed it into a mournful preparation for death. It is a beautiful

symbol of the divine Spirit of life taking possession of the human
body, and breathing into it His vital energy.

"Again, this fundamental principle is most distinctly stated
in the 53rd chapter of Isaiah, as we have seen. Christ is there
said to have 'borne our griefs and carried our sorrows,' the word
'bear' being the very same used for the atonement of sin; the
same used elsewhere to describe the act of the scapegoat in
bearing away the people's guilt; and the same used in the same
chapter with respect to His 'bearing the sins of many.' As He
has borne away our sins, He also bore our sicknesses.

"Peter also states that 'his own self bare our sins in his own
body on the tree . . . by whose stripes ye were healed.' In His
own body He has borne all our bodily liabilities for sin, and our
bodies are set free. That one cruel 'stripe' of His—for the word
is singular—summed up in it all the aches and pains of a
suffering world; and there is no longer need that we should suffer
what He has sufficiently borne. Thus our healing becomes a
great redemption right, which we simply claim as our purchased
inheritance through the blood of His cross.

"But there is something higher even than the cross. It is the
resurrection of our Lord. There the Gospel of healing finds the
fountain of its deepest life. The death of Christ destroys sin—
the root of sickness. But it is the life of Jesus which supplies the
source of health and life for our redeemed bodies. The body of
Christ is the living fountain of all our vital strength. He who
came forth from Joseph's tomb, with the new physical life of the
resurrection, is the Head of His people for life and immortality.

"Not for Himself alone did He receive the power of an endless
life, but as our life. God 'gave him to be the head over all things
to the church, which is his body.' 'We are members of his body,
of his flesh, and of his bones.' The risen and ascended One is the
fountain of our strength and life. We eat His flesh and drink
His blood, and He dwelleth in us and we in Him. As He liveth
in the Father, so he that eateth Him shall live by Him. This is
the great, the vital, the most precious principle of physical
healing in the name of Jesus. It is 'the life also of Jesus manifested
in our mortal flesh.'

"It follows from this that the physical redemption which
Christ brings, is not merely healing, but also life. It is not the
readjustment of our life on the old basis, leaving it thenceforward
to go like a machine upon the natural plane, but it is the im
parting of a new kind of life and strength. Therefore it is as fully

within the reach of persons in health as those who are diseased. It is simply a higher kind of life, the turning of life's water into His heavenly wine.

"Therefore, it must also be kept by constant abiding in Him, and receiving from Him. It is not a permanent deposit, but a constant dependence, a renewing of the inward man day by day, a strength which comes only as we need it, and continues only while we dwell in Him."

Few Christians can read such words as these without being strongly and deeply moved by them. They are brave words, in days of moral cowardice; they are uplifting words, in days of spiritual declension; they are revealing words, in days when the person and power of Christ are greatly obscured. No wonder then, that hundreds and thousands of Christians have found in them comfort, hope and even healing. When a dead Christ is made a living One; when a far-away Christ is made a near One; when an impotent Christ is made an all-powerful One, what other results may follow? And these things Dr. Gordon's and Dr. Simpson's words have brought to pass.

But the question just now is not one of godliness, or courage, or boldness, or convincing power. It is simply this: What, after all, is the truth? That is, were these great teachers wholly right, or only partly right? Were all of their premises scriptural, or also, were some of them unscriptural? And, were all of their conclusions warrantable, or also were some of them unwarrantable? In order to help to a proper conclusion in reference to these important questions, let me attempt to formulate into a condensed statement what Dr. Gordon and Dr. Simpson taught:

1. Sickness resulted from the sin of the fall; so that all sickness is the direct consequence of sin, and special sickness is the result of special sin.

2. Christ came into the world to save men from sin, and from the consequences of sin; and hence, among other things, He came to deliver the Christian from the present, earthly consequences of sin, including physical ill.

3. Christ went to heaven to make good for His saints on earth His redemptive purposes; and as one purpose was to

deliver them from sickness and even physical weakness, to be well and strong is a redemptive right and privilege.

4. The person who brings to the saint God's purposes of grace is the Holy Spirit; and hence, if the Christian receives and holds, by faith, the Spirit in His fulness it will mean to him the fulness of Christ's indwelling, resurrection life, both spiritually and physically.

5. Such being the birthright inheritance of the saint, the Christian has no need of a doctor or medicine; and hence, it is spiritually unjustifiable for him to have recourse to the one or other.

6. These blessings were for the apostles as members of the body of Christ; and as this body is one, irrespective of place and time, what was true for the apostles is true for all other saints.

7. It is, therefore, both the privilege and duty of the Christian, in case of sickness, to send for the elders of the church, to confess every known sin, to be anointed with oil, to offer the prayer of faith, and then to rise up and remain both well and strong.

I shall not attempt, at this juncture, to point out anything which I may deem wrong in the reasoning thus expressed. All I shall do is to set over against the opinions presented by Dr. Gordon and Dr. Simpson quotations from two books which relate to these men of God as they were in their last days, the first volume being, *Adoniram Judson Gordon*, by Ernest B. Gordon, his son; and the second being, *The Life of A. B. Simpson*, by A. E. Thompson, a missionary of the Christian and Missionary Alliance.

Ernest B. Gordon writes of his father as follows:

"There were indications of a coming break, as of a straining beam upon which additional pressure is being constantly placed. His work during the month of January was continuous and intense. One might almost have believed that he was trying to illustrate the proverb. 'The more light a torch gives, the less time it burns.' An idea of his ceaseless activity can be obtained from a mere catalogue of his engagements for the brief two weeks of the sickness which followed. He was to give addresses at

Philadelphia, at Newark, at the mid-winter convention of Dr. Cullis's church, at the conference of the Christian Alliance, Boston, at Mount Holyoke College, and two addresses at Rochester, N.Y. This is addition to his church cares at home. 'I must get out from under these burdens for a little,' he would say. Yet when suggestions were offered and plans perfected for rest he could never be induced to stop. His system was thus depleted and prepared for the entrance of the disease which was to prove fatal.

"Monday, January 21st, was his last day of service. In the evening he attended the annual meeting of the Industrial Home, and went thence to address the Young Men's Baptist Union on the subject of missions. Never did he speak with more delicate humour, with more captivating grace, with greater earnestness; but the lines were deep on his face, as if the graver overwork had been more active than ever, and those who sat near could clearly see that he was far from well. The next day he was unable to leave his bed. The physician was called and the disease pronounced to be grippe, with tendencies to bronchitis. Then for days did he struggle on as in a blinding storm. The fever became violent and was accompanied with intermittent delirium. Night after night he lay in the agonies of a prolonged insomnia. He complained of 'the ceaseless storm, the incessant noise as of great raindrops on a window-pane,' though all the while the air outside was as still as an Indian summer. He would groan at 'the sudden bursts of blackness' which overwhelmed him 'as if he were felled with a club to the ground.' Often in those night hours could we hear him whispering John Angelus' hymn:

> 'Jesus, Jesus, visit me;
> How my soul longs after thee!
> When, my best, my dearest friend,
> Shall our separation end?'

For with all the intense physical suffering there went along a sense of isolation and of desertion. On the Wednesday night before his death this feeling seemed to be overpowering. He asked that every one might leave the room that he might be alone and face to face with Jesus. Then followed such a heartrending confession of unworthiness, such an appeal for the presence and companionship of the Saviour, such promises, with strong crying and tears, of renewed consecration, of greater diligence and devotion in God's service, as are rarely heard. It was as if the Gethsemane prayer were again ascending.

"The next morning it was clear that he was worse. The long period of sleeplessness was fast wearing him out. Toward evening the doctor, coming in, said in a cheery voice, to rouse him from his lethargy, 'Dr. Gordon, have you a good word for us to-night?' With a clear, full voice he answered, 'Victory!' It was as if, after the typhoon-like sickness, he had passed the last range of breakers and had been given a glimpse of the Eternal City gleaming beyond.

"This was his last audible utterance. Between nine and ten in the evening the nurse motioned to his wife that she was wanted. As she bent over him he whispered, 'Maria, pray.' She led in prayer; he scarce followed sentence by sentence, trying at the close to utter a petition for himself; but his strength was not sufficient for articulation. Five minutes after midnight on the morning of February 2nd he fell asleep in Jesus."

A. E. Thompson writes of Dr. Simpson as follows:

"In the following January (1918) he was announced as one of the chief speakers at a Jewish Mission Conference in Chicago, but after the conference had commenced he wired his life-long friend, Mrs. T. C. Rounds, Superintendent of the Chicago Hebrew Mission, who was secretary of the convention, expressing his regrets that he found himself unable to attend. It was a great disappointment, for every one knew that a message for the hour was burning in his heart.

"During the rest of the winter he engaged in very little public ministry, and most of his other duties were laid aside. He submitted to urgent solicitation and, accompanied by Mrs. Simpson, spent a few weeks with his friends of other days at Clifton Springs, New York. He did not, as some have suggested, take medical treatment. Dr. Sanders of the Sanitarium was an old friend and a former attendant at the Tabernacle, and thoroughly understood Dr. Simpson's position.

"When the Annual Council of the Christian and Missionary Alliance assembled at Nyack in May, 1918, Dr. Simpson called upon Mr. Ulysses Lewis, Vice-President of the Society, to preside, though he himself attended most of the sessions.

"Dr. Simpson had lived, as he tells us in the story of his life crisis, a lonely life. One of the secrets of his success was that he had taken his difficulties directly to the Lord, and even his immediate family knew little of the burdens which he bore from day to day. He attempted to continue to meet the pressure that was upon him during the early months of his physical decline as he had always done. The great adversary, against whose kingdom he had so valiantly warred, attacked him in his weakness and succeeded in casting a cloud over his spirit.

"Even yet he did not call his brethren to his spiritual help until one of them, a short time after the Council, asked for the privilege of staying with him at night, at which time the pressure was most severe. For several weeks one or other of the brethren enjoyed what they will ever regard as the unspeakable privilege of this intimate fellowship. He would kneel at his bedside with one who was with him and pour out his heart unto the Lord. After retiring they would lie in sweet communion, quoting the great promises of Scripture and softly singing the hymns which have been endeared to the church, or the yet richer Psalms of David in the old Scottish metrical version, which he, and at least some of these friends, had sung in childhood. When the brother would say, 'Dr. Simpson, you must sleep now,' he would say, 'Yes, yes, but we must have another word of prayer.' By this time that rich consciousness of the indwelling Christ, in which for forty years he had never failed to compose himself for sleep, had returned in some measure to him, and presently he would be sleeping as a child. When he awakened in the morning, addressing the one beside him with the affectionate familiarity of a spiritual father, he would express the hope that he had not disturbed him. Again in 'psalms and hymns and spiritual songs' the day would be begun, till the brother left for his daily duty. So several weeks were passed.

"One day two of the brethren, who had been greatly stirred by the Holy Spirit for his complete deliverance, bowed with him in his library. They prayed a prayer into which he earnestly sought to enter with a real Amen. The brethren knew, as did Dr. Simpson, that they wrestled 'not against flesh and blood, but against principalities, against powers, against the rulers of the darkness of this world, against wicked spirits in heavenly places.' Presently they knew that victory had been given, but they longed and hoped that it also might mean perfect physical deliverance. Before they rose from their knees he said, 'Boys, I do not seem to be able to take quite all that you have asked. You seem to have outstripped me—but Jesus is so real'; and he began to talk to his Lord as only a man who has known the intimate love-life of the Man in the Glory can do.

"Just before the Annual Council in May he suffered a slight stroke of paralysis, which prevented him and Mrs. Simpson from going to Toccoa where the Council was held that year; but he recovered so rapidly that none of the brethren was detained at Nyack. He sent this telegram to the Council: 'Beloved brethren assembled in Council at Toccoa: I regret not being able to meet you this year to look over the blessing of the year gone by. Although turmoil and strife have ruled the world, God has held us by His mighty hand from the many trials and evils which have surrounded us. Blessing has been poured out upon the work and the workers as they have been guided by Him. We praise His name forever. My prayer is that God will rule this blessed work which was begun in sacrifice and consecration to Him, for the spreading of the gospel into all lands. I hope soon to meet you all again as He will. My text to-day is John 11:4—"This sickness is not unto death, but for the glory of God." We are with you in spirit if not in body.'

"On Tuesday, October 28th, he spent the morning on his verandah and received a visit from Judge Clark, of Jamaica, conversing freely, and praying fervently for Rev. and Mrs. George H. A. McClare, our Alliance missionaries in Jamaica, and for the missionaries in other fields, who were always in his mind. After the Judge left him he suddenly lost consciousness and was carried to his room. His daughter Margaret and a little group of friends watched by the bedside with Mrs. Simpson till his great spirit took leave of his worn-out body and returned to God that gave it, early on Wednesday morning, October 29th, 1919."

Let me sum up in a few sentences what we have in these statements, and as I do so, let me add a few facts which have not been quoted above, but are given otherwise in the books mentioned.

1. Dr. Gordon and Dr. Simpson were, at various times, healed of serious diseases; and, beyond doubt, they lived and worked through many years by reason of the physical empowering of Christ.

2. But at times sickness overcame them, and at last final diseases laid hold upon them, grippe, bronchitis and

pneumonia, in the case of Dr. Gordon, and hardening of
the arteries and paralysis of the body and brain in the case
of Dr. Simpson.

3. Both were attended, at the last, by physicians, Dr.
Gordon taking medicine, Dr. Simpson taking none, this last
because the physician said that there was nothing to be done,
which meant that he believed that the disease (arteriosclerosis)
was not subject to medical treatment and was incurable, this
proving to be true.

4. In both cases, much prayer, by the patients themselves
and by hundreds of believing Christians, was offered for
immediate and entire healing, scriptural promises being rever-
ently claimed and spiritual and physical deliverance being
trustingly anticipated.

5. Neither one sent for the elders of the church and neither
was anointed with oil, Dr. Simpson never having been so
anointed.

6. Each one, for a considerable time, fell under a spiritual
cloud, each concluding that he had lost fellowship with God
and was suffering from His displeasure and chastisement.
But each one was finally delivered from spiritual darkness and
was brought back into the light, though this did not result
in prayer for healing being answered and healing being given.

7. In spite of prayer and faith and the ministry of physicians,
nurses and friends, both died.

I shall not comment upon the above findings beyond making
one remark: While no blame is to be attached to these men of
God because of their sickness, suffering and death, yet it is a
fact that there is a wide discrepancy between their final
experiences and what they had taught concerning the Christian's privilege of momentarily and continually deriving his
physical life from the life of the resurrected Christ.

VI

STATEMENTS CONSIDERED

IT is my purpose now, to consider the leading propositions presented in the previous chapter concerning miraculous healing. As the writings of Dr. Gordon and Dr. Simpson present the best, and, therefore, almost the last word to be said in favour of faith healing as generally held, their utterances deserve special consideration.[1] We shall then take up their principal propositions one by one. In quoting, it seems best to refer to the words found in *The Gospel of Healing* as these are similar to those used in *The Ministry of Healing* and they are put in a more analyzed and consecutive form.

"Man has a twofold nature. He is both a material and a spiritual being. And both natures have been equally affected by the fall. His body is exposed to disease; his soul is corrupted by sin. How blessed, therefore, to find that the complete scheme of redemption includes both natures, and provides for the restoration of physical as well as the renovation of spiritual life! The Redeemer appears among men with His hands stretched out to our misery and need, offering both salvation and healing. He offers Himself to us as a Saviour to the uttermost; His indwelling Spirit the life of our spirit; His resurrection body the life of our mortal flesh."

(Gospel of Healing, page 9.)

This, as any one will recognize, is a noble utterance; and it is largely true. But the question arises, is it wholly true? There is no doubt of the fact that Christ's redemption includes man's two natures—indeed, three, spirit, soul and body—and provides for the restoration of the physical life as well as

[1] A clear and forceful presentation of the subject of miraculous healing from the usual standpoint has recently been made by the Rev. Kenneth Mackenzie, in his book *The Divine Life of the Body*, published by the Christian Alliance Publishing Co., New York City.

the renovation of the spiritual. Those who believe in the
resurrection of the body will hold that redemption includes
the body; and those who believe in present-day miracles of
healing will agree that they are the direct result of Christ's
redemptive work and power. But does it follow that Christ
appears among men, in the sense of all saved men and at all
times, with His hands stretched out to their physical need,
offering healing?

Many men, indeed many sanctified and believing men,
have pleaded with Christ for healing and have not received
it. Mr. Hudson Taylor, for instance, who lived through a
long life in almost unbroken fellowship with God and who
trusted Him as few men on earth have done, had few ailments healed in answer to prayer apart from medical aid,
though he was delivered from death again and again with
such aid. With this one case before us, not to speak of the
cases of countless other saints, some of us hesitate to conclude
that Christ stands prepared to heal all Christians at all times,
with its unjust and unhappy implication that Mr. Taylor
and others like him were not healed because they were not
sufficiently holy or did not sufficiently believe. The quoted
statement seems so inclusive in its phraseology as manifestly
to be contrary to experience.

"The earliest promise of healing is in Ex. 15:25, 26: 'There he
made for them a statute and an ordinance, and there he proved
them, and said, If thou wilt diligently hearken to the voice of
the Lord thy God, and wilt do that which is right in his sight,
and wilt give ear to his commandments, and keep all his statutes,
I will put none of these diseases upon thee, which I have brought
upon the Egyptians: for I am the Lord thy God which healeth
thee.' The place of this promise is most marked. It is at the very
outset of their journey, like Christ's healing of disease at the
opening of His ministry.

"God meets us at the very threshold of our pilgrimage with
the covenant of healing, declaring that, as we walk in holy and
loving obedience, we shall be kept from sickness, which belongs
to the old life of bondage we have left behind us for ever.
Sickness belongs to the Egyptians, not to the people of God.
And only as we return spiritually to Egypt, do we return to its

malarias and perils. Nay, this is not only a promise; it is 'a statute and an ordinance.' And so, corresponding to this ancient statute, the Lord Jesus has left for us in Jas. 5:14 a distinct ordinance of healing in His name as sacred and binding as any of the ordinances of the gospel."

(*Gospel of Healing*, pages 11–13.)

Those who have studied prophecy will recognize that God has connected different and contrasted purposes with the various dispensations. For instance, He made Israel a nation and gave them a land, which He has not done for the church. For instance again, He wrought miracles in Israel's behalf, such as making the sun to stand still in the heaven, which he has never wrought in behalf of the church. To argue, therefore, that what God did for His ancient people He will do for His present people, is fallacious and misleading. To illustrate again, out of many illustrations which might be chosen, it says this in Deuteronomy 29:5 concerning Israel, "Your clothes are not waxen old upon you, and thy shoe is not waxen old upon thy foot." Here is a thing which God did in the physical realm and a most easy thing for Him to repeat; and, we might argue, as He loves the church as fully as He did Israel, that He will do now, in respect to clothes and shoes, what He did formerly. This, if it were justifiable, would be a heartening line of thought. But let the Christian, even the holy and believing Christian, "claim the promise" and try to put it into effect, and then see what will happen.

And why will not God respond to the saint now as He did of old, and, for instance, make old clothes and shoes perpetually new? There is but one answer: It is not because He is not able to do so, nor because He does not love now as He did of old, but simply and only because, in respect to such matters, He does not choose to do in this present dispensation what He did in the former. And it is much the same in respect to healing. God made Israel an earthly people and He gave them in a marked way earthly, and, therefore, physical blessings. God has made Christians a heavenly people and He gives them in a marked way heavenly, and, therefore, spiritual blessings. Hence, whatever He now does for the bodies of

Christians, He does, not on the basis of what He did for Israel, but apart from it, in fulfillment of His special purposes of grace in this present dispensation.

"Isa. 53:4, 5: 'Surely he hath borne our griefs, and carried our sorrows . . . and with his stripes we are healed.'

"This is the great evangelical vision, the gospel in the Old Testament, the very mirror of the coming Redeemer. And here in the front of it, prefaced by a great Amen—the only 'surely' in the chapter—is the promise of healing, the very strongest possible statement of complete redemption from pain and sickness by His life and death, and the very words which the evangelist afterwards quotes, under the inspired guidance of the Holy Ghost (Matt. 8:17) as the explanation of His universal works of healing.

"The translation in our English version does very imperfect justice to the force of the original. The translation in Matt. 8:17 is much better: 'Himself took our infirmities, and bare our sicknesses.' The literal translation would be: 'Surely he hath borne away our sicknesses, and carried away our pains.'

"Therefore, as He has borne our sins, Jesus Christ has also borne away and carried off our sicknesses; yes, and even our pains, so that abiding in Him, we may be fully delivered from both sickness and pain. Thus 'by his stripes we are healed.' Blessed and glorious gospel! Blessed and glorious Burden-Bearer!"

(*Gospel of Healing*, pages 15–17.)

The above quotation infers that there was a vicarious element in the healings of the Lord in Galilee, and they argue, since these healings were then and there for all, that this vicariousness, confirmed by the atonement on the cross, makes divine healing now and here for all. This argument seems to be unscriptural. There was no vicarious element in the Galilee healings, Christ not having yet suffered on the cross, and hence universality cannot be founded upon them or deduced from them. Peter in his first epistle gives the divine interpretation of Isaiah 53:4, 5, which Dr. Simpson quotes, in the following words, "Who his own self bare our sins in his own body on the tree, that we, being dead to sins, should live unto righteousness; by whose stripes ye were healed" (1 Pet. 2:24). Here manifestly, the apostle has Isaiah

53:3-5 in mind, and he declares that the meaning of the verses is that Christ bore the burden of our sins not in His life, but in His death "on the tree," that is, on the cross, and that by the stripes, or punishment laid upon Him, there we are healed, or saved. And with this declaration, the other writers of the New Testament agree (Mark 10:45; Rom. 3:25; 5:6-11; 1 Cor. 15:3; 2 Cor. 5:18-21).

We may conclude then that the atonement was wrought out on the cross, and there alone. Nevertheless, we cannot turn aside from the declaration of the Holy Spirit in Matthew 8:17 to the effect that the healings in Galilee were a fulfillment of Isaiah 53:4, 5. This raises the question as to what was the fulfillment which took place. In regard to this, two things are to be noted; first, the Spirit says that the prophecy in Isaiah 53:4, 5 as related to the healings, was then and there "fulfilled," which forbids the thought that it was, in the sense spoken of, fulfilled by the subsequent atonement on Calvary; and second, the context indicates that the fulfillment referred to was related only to healings, and hence had no relationship with sin or an atonement for sin.

It appears, therefore, that Isaiah 53:4, 5 was written with a double prophetic outlook: first to an atonement for sin, of which Peter speaks (1 Pet. 2:24); and second, to the healing of disease, before and apart from the atonement, of which Matthew speaks (Matt. 8:17), this last, undoubtedly, as an evidence and proof of Christ's messianic claim. This double significance, if a rightful interpretation is to be reached, must be kept in view, and the two must be held separate and must not be confused. In other words, Matthew 8:17 does not refer to the atoning work of Christ, and universal healing cannot be founded upon it. It refers to a temporary content connected with the earthly ministry of our Lord, which being "fulfilled" was not to be renewed.

"John 14:12: 'Verily, verily, I say unto you, he that believeth on me, the works that I do he shall do also; and greater works than these shall he do, because I go to my Father.' Here is another: 'Verily,' nay, a 'verily, verily.' Then it must be something emphatic, and something man was sure to doubt. Now, it is no use to tell us that this meant that the church after Pentecost was to have greater spiritual power, and to do greater spiritual works by the Holy Ghost than Jesus Himself did, inasmuch as the conversion of the soul is a greater work than the healing of the body; because Jesus says: 'The works that I do shall he do also,' as well as the 'greater works than these'—that is, he is to do the same works that Christ did, and greater also. And so we know they did the same works that He did."

(*Gospel of Healing*, pages 19, 20.)

This is an instance of generalization, for, as a matter of fact, the apostles, not to speak of subsequent disciples, did not do greater works than Christ, that is, in the physical world. Did any apostle or disciple turn water into wine; or bring up from the sea a draught of fishes; or still a tempestuous lake; or feed five thousand persons with five loaves and two fishes; or heal a man at a distance who was sick and ready to die; or raise a man from the tomb who had been dead four days? Aside from Peter and Paul raising the dead, the apostolic miracles of a physical kind did not approach those which the Lord wrought, either in quality or quantity. One can but conclude, therefore, that the Lord in the words quoted (John 14:12) had reference to acts in the spiritual realm, in respect to which His statement is wholly applicable and true. If this is the case, then they do not refer to acts of healing, and they are not to be made the basis of an assumption to the effect that the apostles and all following Christians may equal and even exceed Christ in His healing power and acts.

"Mark 16:15–18: 'Go ye into all the world, and preach the gospel to every creature. He that believeth and is baptized shall be saved; he that believeth not shall be damned. And these signs shall follow them that believe: in my name they shall cast out devils; they shall speak with new tongues; they shall take up serpents; and if they drink any deadly thing, it shall not hurt them; they shall lay hands on the sick, and they shall recover.'

"Here is the commission given to them, the twofold gospel, and the assurance of His presence and unchanging power. What right have we to preach the one without the other? What right have we to hold back any part from the perishing world? What right have we to go to the unbelieving world and demand their acceptance of our message without signs following? What right have we to explain their absence from our ministry by trying to eliminate them from God's Word, or consign them to an obsolete past? Nay, Christ did give them, and they did follow as long as Christians continued to 'believe' and expect them. For it is important to observe the translation which Dr. Young gives of the seventeenth verse: 'Signs shall follow them that believe these things.' The signs shall correspond to the extent of their faith."

(Gospel of Healing, pages 20–22.)

As will be seen, these words make large claims for the church, and lay down unequivocally the proposition that any Christian who believes may bring to pass the signs spoken of by Christ as recorded by Mark. But these facts are to be noted. A "sign" in Scripture is never a frequent, continuous, or universal event. When the sun rises and sets in its daily course about the earth, it is frequent, continuous and universal, and hence it is not a sign. But when, at the command of Joshua, the sun stood still in the heaven, it was neither frequent, nor continuous, nor universal, and hence, it was a sign. The fact then, that Christ said that these *"signs"* should follow them that believe was the divine indication that they should not be frequent, continuous and universal. In addition to this, what is argued for one of the stated signs must be argued for all of the others; that is, if Christ gave to all believing Christians the right to lay hands on the sick that they might recover, He also gave them the right to cast out demons, to speak with new tongues, to take up serpents, and, if they should drink any deadly thing, to recover. But we do not read that the author of the quotation elsewhere argued for the putting into effect of these other signs of which the Master spoke. He did indeed tolerate seeking for the receiving and exercising of the gift of tongues, during a series of "waiting meetings" at the New York Tabernacle. But this was only for a comparatively short time, for spiritual abuses developed and he brought the meetings to an end. And, finally, it is to be observed that the commission in Mark does not give the right to be healed, but to lay hands on the sick and heal, which two things, though somewhat similar, are distinctly unlike, coming under different classifications and being for different purposes.

"Rom. 8:11: 'If the Spirit of him that raised up Jesus from the dead dwell in you, he that raised up Christ from the dead shall also quicken your mortal bodies by His Spirit that dwelleth in you.' This cannot refer to the future resurrection. That will be by the 'Voice of the Son of God,' not the Holy Spirit. This is a present dwelling and a quickening by the Spirit. And it is a quickening of the 'mortal body,' not the soul. What can this be but physical restoration, which is the direct work of the Holy Ghost, and which only they can receive who know the indwelling of the divine Spirit. It was the Spirit of God that wrought all the miracles of Jesus Christ on earth (Matt. 12:28). And if we have the same Spirit dwelling in us, we shall experience the same works."

(Gospel of Healing, pages 26, 27.)

Those who hold the doctrine of miraculous healing as the right and privilege of all saints make much of this verse in Romans. But before the interpretation which the quotation expresses is given to it, two or three things should be observed. First, the verse does not make the quickening of our mortal bodies dependent upon conditions of any kind, such as the prayer of faith or a sanctified life, as it would do if present experiences were in mind. It simply announces the fact that the Spirit will bring the quickening mentioned to pass. Second, what is promised in the verse is not said to be for a few, peculiarly sanctified and specially believing Christians, but for *all* saints in whom the Holy Spirit dwells, that is, for *every* member of the body of Christ. And third, the verse does not say that the Spirit *now* quickens the mortal body, but that He *will* do so, the difference being between a present and future action. In my opinion, these considerations are insuperable difficulties to making the verse apply to present times and experiences. It seems clear that the words used point forward to the coming of Christ when all who live and believe in Him will be quickened by the Spirit into His form and beauty. It will be of interest to my readers to know that Dr. Gordon, whose miraculous healing views would naturally have led him to an opposite interpretation of the verse than this, told me that a prolonged study of it, including its Greek wording, had forced him to conclude that it could not possibly be made to refer to the present time; and he added that undoubtedly it spoke of the transformation of the body which is to take place at the return of the Lord.

"As a voice that has been speaking for eighteen centuries, let us hear the sweet words (Heb. 13:8), 'Jesus Christ the same yesterday, and to-day, and forever.' And this is but an echo of that voice that spoke these parting words a generation before: 'Lo, I am with you alway, even unto the end of the world.' He did not say, I will be; that would have suggested a break; but I am, an unchanging now, a presence never withdrawn, a love, a nearness, a power to heal and save, as constant and as free as ever, even unto the end of the world; 'Jesus Christ, the same yesterday, and to-day, and for ever.' "

(*Gospel of Healing*, page 28.)

There are few verses in the Word of God more comprehensive in implication and more establishing in effect than the one which is here quoted. It shows, to the comforting and strengthening of the soul, that we have an eternal Christ, who is enduring and unchangeable. The promise, therefore, is a rock foundation upon which to stand and in which to rejoice, through all the events of time as related to oneself, the church, the nations, the world, and the whole universe of God. But, granting this, may one found upon it what the quotation does? Is it true, because Christ is unchangeable in His being and attributes, that also, He is unchangeable in His will and ways? Is He, for instance, doing the same in this church age that He did in the Jewish age, and that He will do in the millennial and eternal ages? To ask these questions is to answer them. The fact is, one of the most blessed things about Christ's unchangeableness is His changefulness. If He were so changeless as to know no change, He would be a machine, not God, nor even man. It is because He is the God-Man, that He thinks and plans, and acts, and so, by various ways and diverse means, brings to pass different purposes at different times. In the nature of the case, therefore, it seems a false line of argument to declare, because Christ healed men in the days when He was on earth, that He will do so now that He is in heaven, and for the simple reason that He is the same "yesterday, and to-day, and for ever." Whether He will or will not heal in our day must be ascertained, not from the standpoint of His eternal sameness, but from that of His revealed will and purpose as related to the present age.

"Jas. 5:14: 'Is any sick among you? let him call for the elders of the Church; and let them pray over him, anointing him with oil in the name of the Lord: and the prayer of faith shall save the sick, and the Lord shall raise him up; and if he have committed sins, they shall be forgiven him.'

"Observe the nature of the ordinance enjoined—'the prayer of faith,' and the 'anointing with oil in the name of the Lord.' Now, this was manifestly not a medical anointing, for it was not to be applied by a physician, but by an elder, and must, naturally, be the same anointing of which we read (Mark 6:13 and elsewhere), in connection with the healing of disease by the Apostles themselves. Any other interpretation would be strained and contrary to the obvious meaning of the custom, as our Lord and His apostles observed it. In the absence of any explanation here to the contrary, we are bound to believe that it was the same—a symbolical religious ordinance expressive of the power of the Holy Ghost, whose peculiar emblem is oil. The Greek Church still retains the ordinance. The Romish apostasy has changed it into a mournful preparation for death. It is a beautiful symbol of the divine Spirit of life taking possession of the human body, and breathing into it His vital energy.

"Again, observe that this is a command. It ceases to be a mere privilege. It is the divine prescription for disease; and no obedient Christian can safely dispense with it. Any other method of dealing with sickness is unauthorized. This is God's plan. This makes faith so simple and easy. We have but to obey in childlike confidence; He will fulfill."

(*Gospel of Healing*, pages 22–25.)

Almost all writers upon the subject of miraculous healing regard the passage in James (5:14–20) as basic and pivotal. Most students of the subject of such healing agree with them

in this, at least in this sense, that it is their opinion that it
is most important carefully to study and accurately to
interpret the passage. But some teachers feel that these last
requirements have not always been fulfilled, and, on the
contrary, that many expositors of the verses have come to
them with biased minds and with the object of confirming
predetermined views. I do not know that I may wholly be
delivered from such a bias of opinion. Nevertheless, I shall
beg to point out certain facts about the passage which often
have been passed by, and which, I think, must be before us
if we are to reach safe conclusions. Let me state these as
follows:

James, as the president of the church council at Jerusalem,
had connection with the church when it was largely Jewish,
both in personnel and character (Acts 15:13-29; Gal. 2:9).

James wrote, not to Gentile Christians, but to Jewish
ones, addressing his epistle to "the twelve tribes scattered
abroad" (1:1).

James wrote to Jewish Christians when they were yet
meeting in synagogues, the words, "If there come into your
assembly," being literally, "If there come into your synagogue" (2:2).

James wrote in a transition period, when the Old Testament
was giving place to the New, and as a Christian Jew to
Christian Jews. He thus continued in part, as Christ did
when He was on earth, the teaching of the Old Testament,
where grace and faith have place (1:6-8), but obedience,
works and visible signs have prominence (1:22-25).

James, in applying Old Testament truths to New Testament conditions, looks upon Christianity, not from the inward
point of view, but from the outward, and thus emphasizes
legal and ceremonial observances. This leads him, among
other similar statements, to define pure and undefiled
religion as visiting the fatherless and widows in their affliction
and keeping oneself unspotted from the world (1:26, 27), a
definition which falls far short of what the Holy Spirit
revealed to Paul who wrote at a later date (Rom. 12:1, 2;
1 Cor. 15:58).

James wrote his letter soon after the Gospels and the Acts

were written and before any of the other epistles were penned.
His epistle, therefore, is the first which was written. For this
reason, it stands, historically and spiritually, just after the
Gospels and the Acts. Hence it links these books with the
later epistles of Peter, John and Paul. It is thus a primary,
midway and partial revelation as between the early Christian
church, where Jewish conditions prevailed, and the later
Christian church, where Gentile conditions prevailed. This
does not ràise the question as to whether or not the Epistle
of James is inspired any more than a similar statement in
respect to the Old Testament or the Gospels would raise the
question as to whether or not they are inspired. The question
is simply one of time, place, meaning and application.

James, it is to be noted, directed those who were sick to
call for the "elders of the church" (5:14). These elders, in the
synagogue congregation, were always men, and were a
formally elected and officially designated ecclesiastical body.
Women, therefore, have no place in this ordinance, nor have
self-appointed independent and unconnected men.

James does not say that the use of means is wrong and
that the physician and medicine are to be excluded, and his
silence, in view of other scriptures which endorse the use of
means, is presumptive evidence that he recognized the place
and service of each. Moreover, it may be assumed that the
cases of sickness which were in his mind were those, in general,
which physicians and medicines could not cure, for otherwise
he would not have turned from them to the church elders,
whose power of healing lay alone in spiritual processes. This
conclusion is confirmed by the fact that Christ and the
apostles chiefly healed, not minor and otherwise curable
diseases, such as toothache, headache, etc., but major and
otherwise incurable ones, such as palsy, blindness, deafness,
dumbness, lameness, insanity and leprosy.

James, I judge, commanded the use of poured-out oil as
a sign and symbol of the poured-out Holy Spirit.   If this
is the case, he thus signified that the Christian patient, openly
and loyally, was to accept the fact that the Holy Spirit was
present, and the additional fact that He was Lord over the
whole being, spirit, soul and body. It was thus an anticipation

and declaration of the truth which Paul expressed, the body for the Lord and the Lord for the body (1 Cor. 6:13). It was under this sovereign overlordship of the Spirit that healing, when granted, was procured and produced.

James affirms that it is the "prayer of faith" which heals the sick (5:15), and he gives an illustration of such a prayer by citing the case of Elijah, who prayed that it might not rain and it rained not, and again prayed that it might rain and it rained (5:17, 18). The apostle thus defines the "prayer of faith" as one which originates in heaven, for Elijah's prayer, before it was offered, was given to him by the Holy Spirit, which fact revealed to him the will of God and thus made him bold to ask for the thing desired. It is manifestly this kind of praying for healing, that is, God-given praying, which produces the recovery of the sick from disease.

James makes it clear that not all sickness is consequent upon and in punishment of particular sin. He says that "the prayer of faith shall save the sick and the Lord shall raise him up" (5:15), which is an unconditional statement. He then adds, "If he has committed sins, they shall be forgiven him" (5:15), which is a conditional statement. That is, a man may be sick and need healing apart from particular sin; or he may be sick and need healing in consequence of particular sin. In the first case, the prayer of faith will obtain healing. In the second case, it will obtain both forgiveness and healing. So we must discriminate between one sickness and another, and we must not assume, because a man is sick, that he has committed some particular sin. Paul confirms this thought in his reference to Epaphroditus, who, he declares, was nigh unto death because of his work for Christ (Phil. 2:30), and who, with all such, was to be held in honour (Phil. 2:29).

Light is thrown upon the James passage by considering the New Testament in general in respect to the use or non-use of oil. There is only one other passage in this part of the Bible which speaks of the use of oil in cases of sickness, namely, Mark 6:13. This reads thus: "They cast out many devils, and anointed with oil many that were sick, and healed them." This quotation establishes the fact that the apostles at times used oil in their acts of healing. But other passages indicate that at other times they did not do so (Acts 3:1–8). It is to be remembered that their using oil, so far as the Word records, was in the lifetime of Christ and thus before the church had been formed. James brings the practice within the time of the church. But again it is to be remembered that he wrote in the early period of the church, during Jewish supremacy. In connection with this, it is to be carefully observed that there is not a passage in the New Testament subsequent to Pentecost which says that the apostles, in cases of healing, used oil, and thus not one which indicates that Paul, the great healer, did so.

This silence of Scripture, as related to the church period and especially as related to its later portion, is suggestive. It seems to indicate that the instructions of James concerning healing were intended particularly for the church in a condition of a large Jewish membership and at a time when it was emerging from Judaism and was spiritually undeveloped; and hence, that they are not so much intended for the church in its present Gentile condition and spiritual maturity. In the last analysis of the case, Paul's writings are to be taken as containing the latest and highest church truth, and it is to be observed that he gives no hint, in his teaching or practice, of sending for the elders in cases of sickness or of anointing by oil. It seems fair to conclude, therefore, that the instructions of James, as related to present-day Christians, are to be regarded as permissive but not mandatory. Dr. Simpson, in spite of his saying that anointing with oil is a command and the divine prescription for disease, seemed to sense the truth of this conclusion, for in his various sicknesses, as already noted, he never sent for the elders of the church and was never anointed with oil.

VII

ARGUMENTS CONSIDERED

It is to be remembered, as I continue this subject, that I have but one object before me. It is not to oppose men; and certainly, it is not to oppose God. My desire is honestly to face facts as they are, both in the Word and experience, and thus to reach sane and solid truth. It is my impression that often those persons who have considered the subject of miraculous healing have been extremists, opposing it *in toto* or else endorsing it *in toto*, when neither the one nor the other is justifiable. It is my hope and prayer to avoid any extreme which may be beyond what is God's revealed truth. If thus, I may set aside the false and preserve the true, then a real gain will have been secured. To this end, therefore, I desire to state in this chapter certain facts which, I think, have sometimes been forgotten, and which, being forgotten, have led to false conclusions and much distress of soul.

A common line of argument in favour of the doctrine of miraculous healing is as follows: Christ came to destroy sin; He came thus to destroy the consequences of sin; sickness is a consequence of sin; and hence, He came to destroy sickness. This seems like unanswerable logic; and indeed it is, for the Scripture confirms each clause of the statement. Nevertheless, a false deduction may easily be made from it, not as related to its objective, but its process. Let me set this forth by a parallel statement, as follows: Christ came to destroy sin; He came thus to destroy the consequences of sin; sinfulness is a consequence of sin; hence, He came to destroy sinfulness. This too seems like unanswerable logic; and indeed it is. But every one knows that its application must be carefully made. For while, judicially, God regards us as sinless (Rom. 5:1), experimentally, He does not do so (1 John 1:8, 10); and we are well aware of the fact that full sinlessness is not to be presently obtained but is only to be secured at the return of Christ, when we shall see Him as He is and be like Him (1 John 3:2). So then logic has its limitations and is to be viewed in the light of revelation and experience. And this is as true of sickness as it is of sinlessness. Christ did die to destroy sickness, and He will yet do it. But He does not say that He will, in a perfect sense, do it *now*, but rather, at a later time, when He comes in power and great glory (Rev. 21:4). The time element is very important, both in prophecy and promise. We need carefully to note, in the one and other, not only what is said, but also when what is said will be brought to pass.

It is argued that if miracles of healing were in Jewish times, also in Christ's times, and also in apostolic times, we may be sure that they may be more than ever looked for in these church times, since Christ has ascended to heaven, been crowned with glory and honour, and now has all power in heaven and on earth. This deduction seems undeniable. But if it is so, just as it is stated, why is not Christ doing now, in the way of miracles, all that He did in the past, and indeed a great deal more? He used to deliver Israel, in times of peril, by lightnings, thunders, hailstones and chariots of fire; why has He not delivered the church, in her times of persecution, in the same way? He fed the hungry multitudes of Galilee with multiplied bread and fishes; why has He never fed the hungry poor of London, New York and the famine-stricken places of China in like manner? He showed His mighty power, even in the days of His earthly humbling, by raising one and another from the dead; why has He never performed, since apostolic days, a single miracle of this kind? He kept Moses alive for one hundred and twenty years, and even then the prophet's eye was not dim, nor his natural force abated; why did He not do the same for the apostles, most of whom died comparatively young, Dr. Gordon, who died at fifty-nine, Dr. Simpson, who died at seventy-six, and Mr. Hudson Taylor, who died at seventy-three? There are evidently great differences between various acts of miracle-working, and, so far as argument is concerned, it appears that more is to be said for the old times than the new. Nevertheless, it is true that

Christ, His redemptive work having been finished and His exaltation having taken place, posesses now more miracle-power than He did in the past. What, then, is to be recognized is this, that, having "all power" (Matt. 28:18), He is not exercising it, in respect to physical miracles, as He did formerly, for His own high and holy reasons. It cannot be argued, therefore, that, because He has at present more power to heal, He will do for the church in healing more than He did for the saints in the past. Indeed, if any deduction is to be made from what He is doing in general, in respect to miracles, He will do now, in healing, not more than He did in the past, but actually less. And the history of the church, even including apostolic times, confirms this conclusion.

The argument of many who hold and teach miraculous healing is to the effect that Christ, by His death and resurrection and by the consequent pouring out of the Holy Spirit, has given to the present-day church all of the gifts which were granted to the apostolic church. But is this so? He gave the apostolic church the gift of inspiration. Has He given this gift to the present-day church? He gave the apostolic church the gift of special miracle working, such as the shadow of Peter healing the sick, and handkerchiefs and aprons from the body of Paul doing the same. Have any such miracles as these been wrought by the members of the present-day church? He gave Peter and Paul power to raise the dead. Has any latter-day saint performed this miracle? The fact of the matter is, there are many miracles which, having been brought to pass in Old Testament and early New Testament times, have never been repeated. This does not mean that the redemptive and pentecostal work of Christ has been undone, or made impotent, or even lessened in power. It simply means that Christ, for His own reasons, is not doing now all that He did in the days of old. So we cannot say that Christ's redemption and ascension and the coming down of the Holy Spirit have brought to the present-day Christians all that they brought to the apostles. On the contrary, judging by the record of the Word as found in the Acts and Epistles, there has been from the first of the church period a diminution in the manifestation of miracles in general, and of acts of healing in particular.

If we are to assume that Christ's commission to perform miracles in the physical realm, as given to the apostles, pertains to us as well as to them, we must conclude that whatever He commanded them, He does us. This assumption, at first sight, is encouraging. But it will be found that it carries us too far. For instance, as previously pointed out, if we are to hold that the sign of Mark 16:17, 18 of laying hands on the sick with the result of recovery is for all believing and Spirit-filled Christians, we must also believe that all of the other signs are for them, that is, that they may cast out devils, speak with new tongues, take up serpents, and drink deadly things without their being hurt; for *all* of the signs are in the same commission and are related to the same persons. For instance again, if we are to assume that Christ's several commandments given to the apostles in reference to performing miracles of healing pertain to us as well as to them, we must be prepared, according to Matthew 10:1-8, not only to heal, but also to exercise power against unclean spirits, to cleanse the lepers and—mark it—to raise the dead. The apostles accepted the commission of our Lord in all of its details, not being staggered by any one of them; and we have the record of various members of the apostolic company performing each of the miracles spoken of, including the raising of the dead. But no one has heard of any modern saint healing all manner of sickness and disease, cleansing lepers, or raising the dead. And the fair assumption is that the Lord's commission of miracle-working as above quoted, was for the apostles alone, they being a special class of men, and hence that it does not apply to the present-day church. We may correctly conclude, therefore, that present-day Christians are not to be classed, in regard to the working of miracles, in the same category as the apostles; and that whatever miracle-power they may be permitted to display is derived from Christ in a wholly different relationship and with an entirely different kind and degree of manifestation.

It is held by many who advocate miraculous healing that it is wrong to make use of a physician and his medicine because the one and the other must necessarily stand between the sick person and God. This means, if such teachers are to be consistent, that they should also hold that means of every sort are wrong, for the same reason. This would bring us to a large conclusion, for we find ourselves dependent upon means of almost every kind and on almost every hand. It is to be admitted, of course, that it is possible for a Christian to make more of a divine gift than the divine Giver. But it need not be so; and with countless Christians it is not so. And some of us find it just as easy to recognize God in the gift of a physician and his remedy as in any other means to a good end. Some Chinese Christians, in taking medicine, bow the head, silently give God thanks for the doctor and his remedy, and ask God's blessing upon the remedy; and many who are not Chinese, in taking medicine, do the same, if not with bowed heads, yet with bowed hearts. In other words, whether or not some particular means will stand between the soul and God, depends, not upon the means, but upon the soul. An irreverent and thankless soul will see the means and not God. A reverent and thankful one will see both the means and God, and God more than the means.[1]

Miraculous healing advocates often make the assertion that the Bible nowhere endorses the use of medicinal means. If this were true, it would not greatly signify, for there are many means to good health which are not commanded by the Word of God but which are commonly recognized as legitimate and useful, such as eating pure food, obtaining sufficient sleep, securing exercise, making sure of proper

[1] Mr. Hudson Taylor, when he went to China in 1853, took his outward journey in a sailing vessel. As he sailed he was greatly troubled. His mother had given him a swimming belt, to use in case of shipwreck. As he thought of the matter, it seemed as if the belt was standing between himself and God, that is, that he was trusting in the belt rather than in the living God. So he gave the belt away. Apparently, it never crossed his mind that the ship upon which he was sailing was a life-preserver of a most effective kind and that he might have made the same objection to it as to the belt. But Mr. Taylor finally thought the matter through and concluded that he was in error. From that time onward, he was conscious that he saw God in means of various kinds as truly and clearly as he did apart from them. (See *The Retrospect*, pages 41, 42.)

sanitation, etc. But, as a matter of fact, the statement is not true. Paul left his companion Trophimus at Miletum sick (2 Tim. 4:20), not healing him, but probably leaving him to the care of a physician and his nursing friends. Also, Paul had a beloved friend and helper named Timothy, who was sick and needed help, and the apostle was moved upon by the Holy Spirit—it is to be remembered that his words are inspired—to advise him in respect to getting well, and it is to be observed that he did not tell him to send for the elders of the church and have himself anointed with oil, as if that were the only permissible thing to do, but wrote, "Drink no longer water, but use a little wine for thy stomach's sake and thine often infirmities" (1 Tim. 5:23), prescribing, as a physician might do, wine as a medicine, as this was then, as it is now, a commonly recognized remedy for stomach troubles, wounds, etc. (Luke 10:34). Moreover, Christ Himself, the great miracle worker and healer, endorsed the use of remedial means. When He healed the blind man, He spat on the ground, made clay of the spittle, anointed the eyes of the blind man with the clay and then told him to go and wash in the pool of Siloam (John 9:6, 7). When He healed another blind man, He spat upon his eyes (Mark 8:22, 23). And when He healed a deaf man who had an impediment in his speech, He put His fingers in the man's ears, and then spat, and touched his tongue with the saliva (Mark 7:32, 33). Now it is to be recalled that Christ healed other blind, deaf and dumb men through no such processes as those mentioned, but simply by a word. Also, it is to be kept in mind that clay and spittle were not in themselves remedies and would not have produced healing. And finally, it is to be remembered that Christ, in His healings, was performing miracles with the purpose of establishing His claim of deity. If, therefore, Christ has utilized remedies for various diseases which were in common use among physicians—though these would not have cured blindness, deafness and dumbness—He would not have wrought a miracle and those who watched Him would have concluded that there was nothing remarkable about the healings, except that the healer was a more clever physician than the other doctors whom they knew. But when He healed without any remedy, and especially when—as appears to be the case—He took such common and non-remedial things as clay and spittle and put healing properties into these, then those who saw were convinced that the healer was none other than their promised Messiah. This, then, is to be noted, that since Christ did put medicinal virtue into the clay and spittle and used these for the purpose of healing physical ills, His action became a solemn, official and divine endorsement of the use of medicinal remedies for the curing of disease.

It seems lawful to some teachers to feel intensely in favour of miraculous healing, and, therefore, to speak harshly concerning physicians and their medicines. For instance, I heard one of the leaders of the healing movement in this country say in a public meeting that a doctor is the "Devil's agent," and that a medicine bottle is a "stink-pot." These statements came rather close home to me, for I have been brought into immediate contact with two medical men—my father-in-law and son—often assisting, in my young manhood, the first one in his surgical operations, and for long observing the second, first on the foreign field and more recently at home, with intimate and intense interest. As related to the former, I have seen brakemen on the Erie Railroad, in western New York, crushed almost beyond recognition by the shunting cars, and have watched the kind doctor, with earnest prayer and the tenderness of a woman, save life, hands, arms and legs. And as related to the latter, I know it as a fact that he never performs an operation without praying, and that he has saved, medically and surgically, hundreds of lives, and, in addition, has helped over five hundred women through the sorrows of childbirth, with the result of not having lost the life of one mother and of only one child. With these two cases pressing upon me, I find it difficult to call either one of them the "Devil's agent" or the bottles which contain their medicines "stink-pots." The Devil is not given to prompting prayer or doing divinely kind and loving deeds; and medicines, while they may smell and taste bad, have a wonderful way, by God's blessing, of working His works and saving imperilled lives. As touching doctors, a certain advocate of miraculous healing said that Luke *was* a physician and that afterwards, ceasing to be a physician, he *became* an evangelist. But the inspired Paul called him "the beloved physician," speaking of him, not as in the past, but as in the then present. As touching medicine, James, the one who exhorted Christians to send for the elders and to be anointed with oil, has this to say, "Every good gift and every perfect gift is from above, and cometh down from the Father of lights" (James 1:17); and I feel assured that these words include medicines, since God Himself called "good" (Gen. 1:12) the mineral and vegetable creation from which remedies are derived.

It is generally held by those who set forth the claims of miraculous healing that sickness is the result of sin—which is true—and that particular sickness is the result of particular sin—which may or may not be true. It is clear, if there had been no sin, that there would have been no sickness; and it is true in the physical world as well as in the spiritual, that whatsoever a man sows, he must reap (Gal. 6:7). At the same time, other reasons than divine judgment may enter into a particular sickness (Job 2:1-8; Dan. 8:27, 10:7-12; Phil. 2:25-30; 1 Tim. 5:23). From the standpoint of the Word, Christ made this plain in the case of the man who was born blind. The superficial disciples asked the Master, "Who did sin, this man or his parents, that he was born blind?" But Jesus answered, "Neither hath this man sinned, nor his parents; but that the works of God should be made manifest in him" (John 9:1-3). And from the standpoint of experience, we have the same lesson set forth, for the spiritual law which prevailed in Old Testament times, namely, that the righteous should be well and the unrighteous should be sick (Ex. 15:26, 23:25; Deut. 7:12-15), does not pertain to New Testament times, as incidents on every hand illustrate. In the old times, the Gentiles suffered physical scourges of all sorts, while the Jews, unless they were disobedient, were kept from such. And as between Jew and Jew, the godly man usually was in better health and lived longer than the ungodly one. But no such distinctions now exist. Epidemics sweep away the unconverted and the converted alike; and frequently, the godly man is more weak and sickly than the ungodly one, while the ungodly one outlives the godly one. The finest physical specimens among men of the present time are prize fighters; and it will be commonly acknowledged, whatever may be said in their favour, that they are not noted for their spirituality. I have in mind a Unitarian who lived to ninety years of age, and his Unitarian sister lived to ninety-seven. I have in mind certain leading scientists who have proved through long years their physical ruggedness and ability to bear strain; but it is said that none of these is a professing Christian and two of them do not believe that there is a personal God. On the other hand, such godly men as George Müller and Hudson Taylor were physically weak, were often sick and died comparatively young. The theory, therefore, that a man is blessed with good health in exact proportion as he obeys God, and suffers from poor health in exact proportion as he disobeys Him cannot be demonstrated in these days, either from the Word or experience. Godliness is profitable, physically and spiritually, for the life that is as well as that which is to come (1 Tim. 4:8). And yet, in spite of godliness, it is evident that there are many times when God chooses that the profit of life shall be other than that of physical health and strength and in the other world rather than in this one.

Some teachers who hold and practice miraculous healing have assumed the attitude that they will not take medicine at any time or under any circumstances, and they consistently hold to their vow of abstinence, however sorely tried they may be by disease and pain. Such persons are to be admired for their desire to please God and their loyalty in carrying out what they believe is right. But a question arises as to their sound judgment, and also, as to their being actually able to fulfil what they seek to bring to pass. As to their sound judgment, let me take this for an example: If you should offer such an one as I have spoken of figs to eat, he would accept them, partake of them, find them helpful to his digestion, and hence, thank God for them. But if a physician should take figs, put them into a press, extract the juice from them, put this in a bottle, mark the bottle "Syrup of Figs," and then prescribe this syrup to the individual, he would refuse the

"drug," and would not give God thanks. It would be difficult
to find consistency in a case of this sort. As to such persons
bringing to pass what they desire, let me present this for
consideration: It is a fact beyond disputing that foods, in
lesser or greater proportion, contain ingredients similar to
those found in medicines. This is true of some meats and many
vegetables.[1] In such cases, the main difference between food
and medicine is that in food the medicinal ingredients are
distributed and in medicine concentrated. A person who
refuses medicine, therefore, is frequently taking it as he par-
takes of the food set before him. Such persons then, while
rejecting medicine and protesting against its use, are almost
constantly living in dependence upon and in benefit from it.
And there would be only one escape from such a condition of
things; it would be necessary to dismiss, not only the physician
and his medicine, but also the cook and her cooking, which is
more than even the average extremist would be willing to do.
In other words, God has inseparably connected our lives with
medicine; and good judgment suggests that we should recognize
this and receive all that God gives to us with thanksgiving. It
is a notable fact that most physicians now recognize the
curative effects of many foods and make it their practice to
prescribe, not medicine but these foods.[2]

There are those who have accepted the doctrine of miraculous healing who make a radical distinction between food and

[1] See, "Food, Nutrition and Health," by Dr. E. V. McCollum, and
"The Newer Order of Nutrition," by Drs. McCollum and Simonds.
The Macmillan Company.

[2] Some time after penning these words I wrote to Dr. Howard A.
Kelly, of Baltimore, asking if my statements were correct. He referred
my letter to the noted specialist upon the subject, Dr. E. V. McCollum,
of Johns Hopkins University. The Doctor's reply was as follows:

"Replying to your letter of October 4, Dr. Frost is right in thinking
that certain foods are so constituted, both qualitatively and quantita-
tively, as to prompt physiological well-being, and a lack of any one
of several principles, e.g. the 6 vitamin, iron, iodine, etc., results in
definite pathological states. Obviously when such conditions result
from taking a faulty food supply the particular foods which are so
constituted as to provide what is necessary may be looked upon
as having a therapeutic effect. The longest known of these is the
antiscorbutic effect of certain fresh vegetable foods."

medicine, accepting the one and rejecting the other. Their argument is that food is constructive and medicine is destructive, and they conclude that physical construction is right and physical destruction is wrong. As a matter of fact, no such distinction between food and medicine may be made, for it is not only true that some foods are constructive and some medicines destructive, but it is also true that some foods are destructive and some medicines constructive. But aside from this, it is impossible to take the position, spiritually or physically, that it is always right to construct and always wrong to destroy. What may be said is that it is always right to construct the good and never right to construct the bad, and always wrong to destroy the good and never wrong to destroy the bad. So the moral quality of one's action, in such cases, is to be determined by its character and purpose. And yet extremists in miraculous healing do not recognize this. They accept food, whatever its effect may be, and reject medicine, whatever its effect might be. Let me illustrate:

Pernicious anemia is a deadly disease. It results from an abnormal condition of the blood-forming organs and of the blood. Blood is made up of red and white corpuscles, healthy blood containing about 5,000,000 red corpuscles to every cubic millimetre, and the ratio of the white to the red being one in five hundred. Anemia, in certain cases, is produced either by this ratio being changed, the red decreasing and the white increasing, or through the chemical degeneration of the red corpuscles. The problem set before the physician, therefore, is to bring back the blood to the normal. To do this, he will make use of sunlight, fresh air and appropriate food, such as liver and kidney substances; and with this the one who believes in miraculous healing will agree. Also, he will seek to re-establish the rightful condition of the blood by the use of iron; and with this many who believe in miraculous healing will not agree. Now, who made the sunlight, fresh air and good food? We answer, God. And who made the iron? We answer, God. And who has authorized us to make distinctions between these means which He has furnished when each and all have been produced by the same Creator and with the same beneficial intent? We certainly, in this case, may not answer, God. On the contrary, in a case of anemia, it is my conviction, since God is in all the four means mentioned, that all should be accepted as from Him and used accordingly. And what is true, as related to anemia, seems to me also true, as related to other diseases, of all other divinely produced means of cure. In respect to the use of iron, it is a strange inconsistency on the part of those who hold to miraculous healing that they would refuse to take iron as a medicine, but would have no hesitancy in eating spinach, in spite of the fact that the latter contains a large proportion of iron and is the present medical treatment in seeking to replenish impoverished blood.

It is taught by some who hold the doctrine of miraculous healing that it is God's purpose to keep the saints in perfect health and strength, and, in case these blessings are lost through disease, to restore them. I remember a gentleman in Toronto whom I asked if he was well. He was an ardent believer in miraculous healing, and for an answer. he threw back his head, squared his shoulders, smote his breast with his hand, and said, "Look at me; Christ is my physical life, and I am in perfect health and strength." He evidently did not quite know himself, for he died within a year. But aside from such a misjudgment, all who claim perfect health and strength speak without knowledge. I mean by this that there is not a man, woman or child living who is in a perfect physical condition. To prove this statement, I have but to ask one or two questions. Adam, before the fall, was perfectly well; are we as well as he? The patriarchs lived for hundreds of years; do we live as long as they? Judged by the standards thus set up, the present generation of mankind, including all who hold miraculous healing, falls far short physically of what has been and, ideally, should be. So then "health" and "strength" are, at best, comparative terms, with the comparison against us.

In addition to the foregoing, this is to be noted. The scientists of the Rockefeller Institute, New York City, have demonstrated beyond doubting that all persons, young and old, rich and poor, well and unwell, are indwelt by tubercular germs, and that the struggle of existence with every one is to keep himself in such a physical state as to prevent these germs from developing to that degree as will give them mastery and control of the physical system. To prove this, one could take an entirely well person, who has no history or taint of tuberculosis about him, put him in a damp place, take away sunlight, pure air and good food, and ultimately that person would develop the disease, and it would come, not from without, but from within. So when we speak of a person as well, we must necessarily use the word, not accurately but inaccurately, not exactly but loosely. That is, one person is well as compared with another who is not well; or a person is well as compared with what he was when he was sick. But as for a person being absolutely well as compared with the unfallen Adam—to take him as a standard of good health—there is not a person living who can lay claim to being this. And this was as true in the Lord's time as it is now. And it was as true of those whom He healed from specific disease as it was of those whom He did not heal. So then, disease, as related to mankind, is universal; and even in a case of actual miraculous healing, it is, strictly speaking, partial and not total. It is for this reason, amongst other things, that the Spirit speaks of "the body of our humiliation" (Phil. 3:21) and says that "we groan within ourselves, *waiting* for the adoption, to wit, the redemption of our bodies" (Rom. 8:23).

The claim is made by some that good health may be the portion of each Christian because it is his privilege to receive and exercise the power of the resurrection-life of Christ; and it is pointed out that this power, being perfected by the atoning death of Christ and His subsequent exaltation to the place of authority at God's right hand, is beyond anything which the saints had previous to Pentecost. Half truths are dangerous things; and even full truths are, when they are misapplied. This is a case of a full truth; and I think its danger is in its misapplication. To substantiate this statement let we point out a few scriptural facts. The apostles after Christ's resurrection drew mightily upon His power; yet not one of them did the miraculous things which the Master did before He was resurrected, that is, of the same kind—except in the raising of the dead—or in the same measure. Peter never turned water into wine; he never stilled a tempest; he never—so far as we know—healed a leper; he never bade anyone walk on the water; he never fed multitudes with five loaves and two fishes. In fact, his miracles, even his miracles of healing, were comparatively few. And what was true of Peter was even more true of Paul. As to the other apostles who lived after Pentecost, excepting John in a single instance, the record says almost nothing of their miracle working. And as to any of them having abounding health and strength, there is absolutely nothing said in the New Testament about this, which seems to indicate that they lived physically as other men lived. In the case of Paul, we have indications from his writings of his physical condition. But he, who knew more about the resurrection power of Christ than any other apostle, set forth in several statements the fact that he was often far from well (2 Cor. 1:8, 9; 4:8–12; 11:24–27; 12:7–10). In addition, if the resurrection increased Christ's right to display His power and increased the power which was to be displayed, how is it to be explained that He performed more and greater miracles before His resurrection than He did or has done after it? And if the saints may know more of God's miracle power now, because of Christ's resurrection and ascension, how is it, to take a single example, that they do not live as long as the patriarchs of old lived who knew nothing of Christ's resurrection life? As far as I can tell, there is but one way in which to answer the above questions. It is true that Christ has taken to Himself more power than He had before the resurrection and that He has displayed this more since that event than before it; but it has pleased Him to express this in the spiritual world rather than in the physical. It does not follow, therefore, that the saints now have the right to go beyond the miracle positions of the saints of old. The fact of the matter is, the very reverse of this is true.

Many who hold the doctrine of miraculous healing state that the Holy Spirit who proceeds from the resurrected Christ, brings the fulness of the life of Christ to the saint, and that this life, through faith on the part of the recipient, may become, not only his spiritual life, but also his physical one, so that the individual may enjoy, during all of his days on earth, the fulness of physical life. Here is the danger of a half truth, not, as in the preceding instance, of a full one. It is wholly true that the Holy Spirit proceeds from the resurrected Christ and that a saint may be filled with Him; but it cannot be proven either from the Word or experience that every one who is so filled has a fulness of physical life. Eliminating the verse which is made so much of, namely, Romans 8:11, which appears to have nothing to do with our present experiences (see pages 62, 63), there is not a passage in the New Testament which proves that the Spirit stands ready at all times, in all circumstances and through the length of life to give abounding health and strength to Christians. And the history of the church, while it has notable examples of those to whom the Spirit has given exceptionally good health for the fulfilment of some special service, records that in all cases there has been a final physical breakdown which has resulted in death, and also, that there has been an almost countless number of devoted and trustful men and women who have fulfilled through life their earthly mission through the "much tribulation" of physical infirmity.

A friend once spoke to me about Dr. Simpson, and declared that he certainly drew his physical life from the Holy Spirit. I did not deny the statement, but I did venture to say one word. It was this: "Wait!" And neither of us had to wait long, for a few years later, the good Doctor went to pieces, physically, and, because of his physical ailment, spiritually; and, while he was restored spiritually, he was never recovered physically. Few who know the Holy Spirit will deny that He has power to maintain one in health and strength. But such persons need to be careful not to go too far in their deductions, for it is evident that the Spirit has set limitations upon Himself as to what He will presently do for the bodies of the saints, both as related to the church at large and the individual members of it. Moreover, it is manifest that He has no fixed rule by which He works, for He deals with each person according to His infinite knowledge of what is right and best for him (1 Cor. 12:4–11).

Teachers of miraculous healing who set forth the doctrine of perfect health and strength because of an infinite Holy Spirit, reach a place of difficulty before they are done with the subject, which sometimes makes them to have recourse to strange explanations. I refer to the fact that death, previous to the second coming of Christ, is universal (1 Cor. 15:51; Heb. 9:27). As to this, it is to be noted, just as the fall of Adam has no place in the theory of evolution, that death has no place in the theory of physical life in the Spirit. Grant that God, the Holy Ghost, may be at all times our physical life, we must conclude, in all consistency, that we need not die, since the Spirit is an "eternal Spirit" and never dies (Heb. 9:14).

Dr. William J. Erdman once asked Dr. Simpson why, according to his teaching, a saint had to die, and the Doctor was honest enough to say, "I do not know." And yet, when Dr. Simpson wrote his book on miraculous healing (*Gospel of Healing*, pages 66, 67), he had recourse to this language, it being, with the facts before him, the best statement which he could make: "When the end comes, why need it be with painful and depressing sickness, as the rotten apple falls in June from disease and with a worm at the root? Why may it not be rather as the ripe apple would drop in September, mature, mellow, and ready to fall without a struggle into the gardener's hand?" As a matter of fact, though Dr. Simpson did not intend it to be so, this is spiritual camouflage. For the illustration used is the covering up of the ugly truth that death is an enemy; that he insidiously lays hold of saint and sinner alike; that he brings disease of some sort, sooner or later, upon all; and, finally, that he gives the fatal grip, and the individual, no matter what his prayer and faith may be, dies. So the time comes, universally, when the theory of physical life in the Spirit breaks down and fails. Dr. Simpson found it so, and his last sickness and final death were anything but like the dropping of an apple in September into the gardener's hand. The same is true of Dr. Gordon and Dr. Cullis. Indeed, in varying circumstances, the same has been true of all the saints who have lived and died. And it will be true—until Christ comes—of all other saints. The Spirit of the resurrected Christ may quicken us, but it is certain that He will never give us resurrection bodies until the resurrection time has come (1 Cor. 15:51–57; 1 Thes. 4:13–17).

There is an aspect of this subject which, I think, most miraculous healing teachers fail to recognize, and which, this being the case, leads to a measure of blindness in respect to the true proportions, values and objectives of life. Let me make plain what I mean by asking two questions: First, is it so important that a saint should always be well and strong and active? And second, is it so desirable that a saint should always live to a good old age?

As touching the first, there may be no doubt as to what our natural desire is, for we do not like disease, weakness and pain; and I fear that this natural desire has much to do with the fervency of our prayers and the urgency of our faith in seeking good health and healing. But is not an insistence upon freedom from disease a going back to the days of Israel, who were children in position and experience and for this reason could not and would not endure suffering? And is not the bearing of physical affliction, when it is needful, the maintaining of our high position as Christians, proving that we can be weak and yet strong, that we can sorrow and yet rejoice, that we can be chastened and yet not misunderstand, and that we can suffer and yet praise? Paul reached his highest attainment, not through perfect health, but in just such a process of physical loss and spiritual gain as this (2 Cor. 4:7–11); and we shall do well, if God so appoints, if we follow in his steps.

As touching the second, it is not strange that the Old Testament saints desired long life and a good old age, for they had no heaven and Christ, as we have, to go to at death (Psa. 88:3–6, 10–12). But for a New Testament saint to wish to lengthen out his days interminably, suggests that he knows little about the city whose builder and maker is God, or about the Lamb which is the light thereof. I suppose the young Paul desired to live as long as possible. But one day he had a vision of heaven and Christ, and from thence he was in a strait between staying—for the sake of others—and going— for his own sake—knowing that going was "very far better" (Phil. 1:23, R.V.). It would not be right to seek sickness or death. But it is right to seek to be careful not to lay such an undue emphasis upon the present life as to make us prefer it to the life which is to be. And this thought suggests that one object which God, at a given time, may have in allowing disease and sickness to come and in not answering prayer for healing and health, is to give us a right perspective as between earth and heaven, and thus to make us to be willing and even long to be absent from the body and at home with the Lord (2 Cor. 5:8; Phil. 1:20–23).

VIII

DIVINE MIRACLES

A MIRACLE is supernatural; but it is not unnatural. A miracle is above law; but it is not opposed to law. A miracle is God working on a plane familiar to Himself, but unfamiliar to men, which, transcending human thought and explanation, becomes to men a wonder, marvel and sign.

It follows that a miracle is God's opportunity to display, first, what He is in Himself, and second, what He is as compared with men. It demonstrates the fact that He is all-powerful and good; and it makes it plain that He is more powerful and good than any man. The continuation of miracles, therefore, is proof to men that there is one God, that He is from overlasting to everlasting, that He is Almighty and that He is full of truth, wisdom and grace.

The miracles of the Old Testament had in them these divine qualities and purposes; and they often produced the effects designed. They revealed God to the ancients—the Scriptures not having been written—as no other acts of His could do; and those ancients feared, revered and worshipped Him accordingly. The ten plagues in Egypt had this beneficent design in them as related to the Egyptians; and they only turned into judgments upon that people as they failed to discern and accept their intent. The miracles of the wilderness were meant to induce the Jews to believe that they had with them a near, a powerful and a loving God, and to confirm and develop their belief in Him.

When God commissioned His prophets to perform miracles, He had the foregoing objects concerning Himself in view. But additionally, He had the design of establishing His servants before men as those whom He had sent, and thus, as those who had the duty and privilege of speaking in His behalf. The miracles wrought by Elijah and Elisha were of this character, and they produced the intended results. They

87

demonstrated God, so that the two prophets were feared as those who possessed the power of God and were revered and heeded as those who had the right to speak for God. Miracles, then, were the signs of God's presence with the prophets and the credentials of their calling. Generally speaking, when new prophets were sent to Israel, they made clear their appointment and authority by new miracles. It is to be noted, however, that the miracles of the Old Testament were comparatively few in number, and that these few were scattered over a long space of time, there being recorded but fifty in all and these being distributed through a period of about four thousand years. It is to be noted also, that many of these miracles—aside from raising the dead and making the sun to stand still—were comparatively simple in quality, these being related, for the most part, to the objects of nature rather than to the lives of mankind. Among the fifty individual cases recorded—aside from the case of the multitudes healed by looking at the brazen serpent—there are only three which had to do with the healing of the body.

The New Testament miracles are to be divided into two classes: first, those which Christ wrought when He was on earth; and second, those which He wrought, through the apostles and a few others, after He had ascended to heaven. From a general standpoint, they had the same purposes as did the Old Testament ones, that is, they revealed the presence, power and beneficence of God, and they corroborated the claim of those who performed them that they were His authorized and accredited representatives.

In addition, the miracles of Christ, as compared with those of the prophets and apostles, had about them, besides their general character, a particular and unique quality, for they were designed to prove that He was the Messiah, that is, that He was the One who, in Old Testament times, had been spoken of by the prophets, and hence that He was on earth as the fulfillment of the promise that God would dwell among men (Isa. 53:4; Matt. 8:17, 18; 11:2-5; Acts 2:22).

As the promised Messiah, Christ was related to the natural world and to humankind; to the world as its creator and preserver, and to men as their redeemer, sanctifier and benefactor.

These relationships were before Christ in all of His earthly ministry, and designedly and peculiarly in the miracles which He wrought. With the first objective in mind, He began His miracle-working with a nature miracle, turning water into wine; and He continued it with other nature miracles such as stilling the tempest and multiplying the bread and fishes. With the second objective in mind, He began by healing the nobleman's son; and He continued such manifestations through the years by casting out demons, healing the sick and raising the dead.

Christ seems to have performed only two miracles in the first year of His ministry, the greater part of them being wrought in the second and third years. But in this later time He rapidly multiplied these signs, there being no fewer than thirty-five recorded. Moreover, He compressed all of His miracles into the short space of less than three and a half years. He thus went far beyond all previous and subsequent miracle-workers, which was consistent with His high and unique claims.

It is to be noted that most of Christ's miracles had to do with the bodies of men, either from the standpoint of maintaining life, such as providing food, or from the standpoint of healing disease, such as casting out demons, making the blind to see, the deaf to hear, the dumb to speak and the lame to walk. Christ did not perform one miracle upon men in judgment. On the contrary, the element of compassion predominated, this entering into all of the miracles which were wrought. But compassion was not the first or largest element in Christ's miracle-working. His main purpose was to establish the fact before God, angels and men that He was indeed the promised Messiah (Matt. 8:16, 17). This explains the message which He sent to John in prison when the prophet had come to doubt His personality and authority (Matt. 11:2–6).

These last statements are important as related to physical healing. If compassion was the main purpose of Christ in performing miracles, then we may argue that there is as much need of compassion now as in the past, and may anticipate the same evidences of it as previously. If, on the other hand, the main objective which Christ had before Him was to prove that He was what He claimed to be, namely, the Son of God, then we must conclude, He having given His proof and substantiated His claim, that the special need of His working miracles, including those of healing, passed away. This is particularly true of the time which eventually followed when the Gospels had been written and had been put into the hands of men, for then there were before them the facts of Christ's miracle-life, which was all the evidence that was needed of what He had been and was as the Son of God.

In considering the miracles of healing which Christ performed, several things are to be observed. First, Christ's healings were related to diseases which were more or less peculiar to His time and the country in which He lived, there being a decidedly ancient and Palestinian character to some of the diseases described, as, for instance, leprosy, which is now comparatively rare in civilized lands; and secondly, they were related to diseases which were beyond the power of physicians to heal. This last is specifically stated concerning the case of the woman who had the issue of blood (Luke 8:43–48); and it is implied in other cases, because the diseases, such as blindness, deafness, dumbness, leprosy, lunacy and demon possession, were manifestly beyond any remedial skill which was known to men in those early times, as they are largely beyond such skill now.

To accept as true, even in part, the foregoing statements is to establish an important principle in Christ's procedure in acts of healing. He chose chiefly those cases for healing which would show His infinite tenderness and mercy by giving healing to those whom men could not heal, and also He chose those which would specially reveal His pre-eminent power as compared with man's comparative impotence. These two facts explain, in reference to healings, the omissions of the Gospels as well as their statements, for it is to be noted that there is not an intimation in them that Christ did what men could do, namely, set broken bones, fill decayed teeth, correct impaired eyesight where glasses were sufficient, take away headaches, relieve rheumatic and neuralgic pains, etc. It is a great principle with God, that He allows men in all things to do for themselves and their fellowmen what they can do, and, usually, that he steps in and displaces them only when their ability and power have come to an end. This, apparently, was the principle which governed Christ in what He did and did not do in His earthly acts of healing. He allowed the physicians of the day to heal where they could heal; and where they had tried and failed, or where they were, in the nature of the case, unable to act, He demonstrated, at such times, places and ways as He chose, His compassion and deity by healing those who were otherwise incurable.

When we come to the healings wrought by the apostles, two things become apparent; first, we pass out of the sphere of Christ's unique relationship to miracles, since the apostles, being only men, were not called upon to manifest personal deity (Acts 3:1-6, 12; 14:8-18); and second, we revert to the sphere of relationship which the Old Testament prophets had, since also, being but men, they were not called upon to manifest personal deity (Ex. 7:1-5; 11:1-10; Dan. 2:27, 28). This makes it plain that the purpose of Christ in working miracles through the apostles had a twofold objective, namely, the continued manifestation of His divine power and goodness, and also the giving of indisputable evidence of the apostles' divine calling and mission. This was the conception which the apostles themselves had of their empowering for miracle-working, including healing, and the claim for themselves which they made before men (Mark 16:15-20; Rom. 15:18, 19; 2 Cor. 12:12).

The above will explain several things in connection with the miracles which the apostles wrought. In reading the record of the Acts, as compared with that of the Gospels, we see a great change in respect to miracles. First, they largely diminish in frequency, and secondly, they alter considerably in kind. The miracle of raising men from the dead runs like a golden thread from the beinning to the end of miracle-working as recorded in the Scriptures, bringing the miracle-acts into unity as to their one source and common purpose. But, aside from the display of this supreme power, the apostles, like the prophets, never duplicated or even approached the record of Christ. He, in His own person and in the short space of three and a half years—I speak of the record as given in the Gospels —performed thirty-five miracles; while a dozen apostles in the course of over thirty years—I speak of the record as given in the Acts—performed about ten.[1] It is to be noted that no apostle performed a nature miracle, such as turning water into wine and multiplying bread and fishes, these being reserved for the divine Christ. They were all, besides the two cases of raising the dead, miracles of bodily healing. And here, also, the diseases, as far as the details are recorded, were beyond the healing power of the medical men of that day. It may be concluded, therefore, that the apostles performed comparatively few miracles, and, like their Master, abstained from healing where men could heal, displaying the power committed to them only where physicians were unable to help. This last made their miracles the more effective from the evidential standpoint.

It is to be kept in mind that Christ gave power to the apostles to perform miracles, as had been the case with the prophets, in order to establish them in the confidence of those persons who saw their acts and heard their messages. Also, it is to be remembered that the need of this accrediting, the power having been displayed and the confidence having been obtained, passed away in the passing away of the apostles. And, again, it is to be kept in mind that there cannot be a recurrence of apostolic miracles—whatever else God may grant—because the apostles as a class have ceased to exist, and also, because there is no present need of these as the inspired New Testament is in men's hands and they have the record in it of the apostolic signs. And, it is to be noted that this is as true of miracles of healing as of any other kind. If, therefore, a miracle of healing at any present time is brought to pass, it may be known at once that it is not an

---

[1] This citation of figures does not represent the total of the healings which were wrought by Christ and the apostles. On the contrary, the Scriptures declare that there was a large number of such which were not specifically described (Matt. 8:16; Acts 2:42, 43; 5:12-16). But we may conclude that the Spirit had a purpose in specifying the cases which He did, both as to their number and kind, and that thus He sought to establish a comparison between the miracle-work of Christ and that of the apostles.

apostolic one, in the sense that Christians are the successors of the apostles, or that they have inherited from them their miracle-power, or that they have miracle-power because they had it. Christ was unique as the Son of God, and hence displayed His miracle-power solely from His standpoint and as related to Himself; and the apostles, including Paul, were unique as those who had seen Christ and were commissioned to establish the church, and hence they displayed their miracle-power solely from their standpoint and as related to themselves. But present-day saints are in a later and lower official order, and hence whatever miracle-power they may display is from their standpoint and as related to themselves. And this brings us to the following deduction: Christ had the greatest place and needed the greatest confirmation, and thus He displayed the greatest miracle-power; the apostles had a lesser place and needed a lesser confirmation, and thus they were required to display a lesser miracle-power; and we have a still lesser place and need a still lesser confirmation, and thus we are required to display a still lesser miracle-power.

If these statements are true, the decrease of miracle manifestation, first, subsequent to the time of Christ, then subsequent to the days of the apostles, and finally, during the period of the post-apostolic church, will readily be understood. As a proof of this thought, I would call this to mind: Christ raised men from the dead; two of the apostles, Peter and Paul, also raised men from the dead; but no saint, from the apostolic time to this, has ever raised any one from the dead; and again, Christ cleansed many lepers; we have no record of any apostle cleansing a leper; and certainly no man since the apostles has ever cleansed a leper. And this is to be particularly noted: the reason for the lessening power, as between the apostles and later disciples, is not to be explained by saying that there has been a spiritual decline from apostolic days to these, so that none has been holy as the apostles were holy and none has believed as they believed; it is to be explained rather by the sovereign choice of God and the peculiar official position, accredited by appropriate gifts, which He designed and permitted the apostles to hold (Acts 5:15; 19:11, 12). The apostolic miracles, therefore, were the divine sign to mankind that God had chosen the apostolic company as Christ's special representatives and messengers. It follows, for this reason, that their miracles of healing are not necessarily to be repeated.

In addition to the foregoing, it is to be kept in mind that both Christ and the apostles had the definite mission before them of offering the messianic kingdom to the Jews. The Old Testament prophets had made promises of many and large physical blessings to the Jewish people when the kingdom should come. Christ and the apostles, in proclaiming the kingdom, made good the words of the prophets by fulfilling the promises of physical blessing which they had made. This explains why most of the New Testament miracles of Christ were wrought in the second year of His ministry, which was that of His general popularity and acceptance. This also explains why these miracles diminished in the third year of His ministry, which was that of His gradual and final rejection. This also explains why there was a recrudescence of miracles in the early years of the apostles' ministry, and a diminution of them as their ministry continued. In short, the miraculous acts increased to the degree the Jews accepted Christ and decreased to the degree they rejected Him. When the Jewish nation had finally rejected Christ, as also the apostles, Stephen and Paul, miracles, including miracles of healing, almost ceased. What remained were isolated acts which corroborated the apostolic authority and continued the witness to a living and loving Christ. When the time comes for a new offering of the kingdom to Israel, miracle-working will be renewed (Rev. 11:3–6); and when the kingdom has been established all of the prophetic promises concerning miracles, including healing, good health and long life, will be fulfilled. But now, the kingdom is not being offered to the Jews, for this is the church age. It is not, therefore, the age of miracles, except as God is pleased to manifest His power to individuals, in exceptional circumstances and for specific purposes.

As to the apostles living in the fulness of health and strength, there is no scriptural evidence of this. The silence of the Scripture in this respect indicates that their lives were lived out on a natural plane. It is probable that all of them, as

Paul said of himself, were men "appointed unto death" (1 Cor. 4:9). And it is reasonably certain, as the Scripture intimates and tradition affirms, that each one, excepting John, was chosen for a comparatively early ending of life and, at the end, for the peculiar suffering of a martyr's death. The traditions to this effect are tersely brought together in *The Bible Handbook*, by Dr. Joseph Angus:

"Matthew suffered martyrdom by the sword in Ethiopia. Mark died at Alexandria after being dragged through the streets of that city. Luke was hanged on an olive-tree in Greece. John was put into a cauldron of boiling oil but escaped death, and was banished to Patmos. Peter was crucified at Rome with his head downwards. James was beheaded at Jerusalem. James the Less was thrown from a pinnacle of the temple, and beaten to death below. Philip was hanged against a pillar in Phrygia. Bartholomew was flayed alive. Andrew was bound to a cross, whence he preached to his persecutors till he died. Thomas was run through the body at Coromandel in India. Jude was shot to death with arrows. Matthais was first stoned and then beheaded. Barnabas was stoned to death by Jews at Salonica. Paul 'in deaths oft,' was beheaded at Rome by Nero."

IX

CHRI'STS SOVEREIGNTY

THE sovereignty of God is not a doctrine which appeals to the natural man. Indeed, it is repellent to him because it creates a situation which is beyond his understanding and control. Few of us take readily to the thought of surrendering our lives into the hands of another, even though that other is God. We prefer to reserve to ourselves the right of choice and thus to limit others to the right of advice. We shrink from autocracy and dogmatism, whether it is human or divine.

In no aspect of life is our human foolishness more manifest than when we assume such an attitude toward God. "God is light" (1 John 1:5) and "God is love" (1 John 4:8), and what more can any soul want in Him than this? If our heavenly Father's love is controlled by wisdom, and His wisdom is expressed in love, we have our sufficiency in Him. But, often, we believe in ourselves—our wisdom and love—more than in Him. Hence we are inclined to deny Him His sovereign choice and acts.

This affects ourselves, to our great and permanent loss. But it does not affect God. Whether we approve or disapprove, "He doeth according to his will in the army of heaven, and among the inhabitants of the earth" (Dan. 4:35). From the beginning it has been so. To the end it will be so. And happy it is, for this earth and all men in it, that it is so. for otherwise, there would be infinite and eternal chaos.

These remarks are not aside from the subject before us, but have a direct bearing upon it. For nowhere has God's sovereignty been more pronouncedly shown than in the world of miracle-working, including the miracle of healing the body. Because this is so, I now purpose to set forth the fact in several paragraphical statements. In doing this, I shall concentrate my thought upon the person of Christ, speaking of His sovereign will and ways.

Christ was sovereign in respect to the time in which He came to earth. It was several thousand years after man's creation before Christ came to serve mankind in redemption and sanctification. During that time, many generations of people came and went, which involved the living and dying of millions of men, women and children. We may take it for granted that the majority of these, during their lifetime, developed physical infirmities, and we know that all of them —with the exception of Enoch and Elijah—eventually passed into physical debility and death. And yet, in all of these thousands of years, Christ remained in the glory, looking upon this infinite woe, and doing practially nothing of a miraculous kind for the alleviation of man's physical pains and sorrows. It is true that He gave Israel a perfect sanitary code. But this was on a natural line of things, and also, it had almost no application to the world at large, so that the vast majority of men lived and died without more medical and surgical help than that which human-minded physicians could give. At last Christ came, in what Paul called "the fulness of time" (Gal. 4:4). But this time was sovereignly chosen by Christ.

Christ was sovereign in the race of people with which He identified Himself. No human reason can be given why Jesus should have been born a Jew. Many divine reasons, of course, may be stated, such as those which are connected with God's prophecies, promises and purposes. But otherwise, our Lord might have been born of any other godly virgin mother than Mary, and have lived as some other person than a Jew. Indeed, from our Gentile standpoint, we might well argue against a Jewish and in favour of a Gentile birth, and our argument would be strengthened by the fact that Gentiles have always vastly outnumbered the Jews. But Christ did not consult men in the matter. What He did was to exercise a sovereign choice. Hence, the Scriptures set before us a virgin who was descended from Abraham and David; and hence they present to us Jesus, the seed of David and the heir of David's throne.

Christ was sovereign in the choice of the land of His nativity and earthly living. Granting that Jesus was to be a Jew, it is not to be concluded that there are any human reasons why Jesus should have been born in Palestine. The Jews were a widely scattered peoole at the time of Christ's birth, the most learned, wealthy and influential among them being in other countries than the Holy Land. We might argue, therefore, for say, Alexandria, or Babylon or Rome as a birthplace rather than the little village of Bethlehem. But Christ did not ask men where He should be born. He had said, "Thou, Bethlehem, in the land of Juda, art not the least among the princes of Juda; for out of thee shall come a governor, that shall rule my people Israel" (Matt. 2:6); and hence, on one blessed night, the Babe lay in Bethlehem's manger. It was a case of a sovereign choice.

Christ was sovereign in the places He visited. As to Palestine, it is the general impression that Christ covered in His itineraries the whole of that land. But this is far from true. It is impossible to mark out with exactness the journeys which He took; but this may be done approximately. Doing this last, reveals the fact that Jesus kept mostly to beaten paths, going to and fro between Galilee and Judea, between Capernaum and Jerusalem. As to Gentile lands, in all of the space of His earthly service, He kept Himself from these, touching only, and that but once, the nearby coasts of Tyre and Sidon. The result of this geographical exclusiveness was that a comparatively small portion of Palestine was visited, and that the greater part of its multitudes was left untouched; and also that the great Gentile nations, stretching far away eastward and westward and having uncounted millions of people, never saw His face, nor heard His voice, nor felt His healing touch. Therefore, to say, as a certain teacher does, that Christ's healing ministry on earth was universal is far from the facts of the case. It was universal so far as individual villages and districts in Palestine were concerned, that is, at the time He was there; but otherwise, it was restricted both in space and time. In other words, Christ sovereignly chose where He would journey and where He would demonstrate His miraculous power. He was the master of His own plans and ways, never asking even the apostles where He should go or what He should do. He was thus continually sovereign in His decisions and actions.

Christ was sovereign as to the people whom He healed. Inasmuch as Christ did not go everywhere, He did not heal everybody. This is true of certain parts of Palestine as compared with certain other parts; and it is true of the whole of Palestine as compared with the whole world. Jesus, therefore, established great differences in respect to healing between persons and persons, showing mercy to some and withholding it from others. Taking the largest possible view of Christ's healing acts and counting these, not by the score, but by the hundreds or thousands, we must recognize that what He did in the way of healing was infinitesimal in comparison with the perhaps three millions of people in Palestine and the perhaps eight hundred millions of people scattered abroad on the face of the earth. In other words, if compassion for the multitudes in connection with their physical condition was the chief constraint upon Jesus in His healing acts, His life and ministry must remain an enigma, for these were not widely effective. And if we reduce the problem from the world at large to the saints in the world, the enigma remains, for the disciples in a short space of time were greatly increased and widely scattered abroad and Christ never went to them in person, nor did the apostles reach any considerable number of them. This brings us back to Christ's sovereignty. His chief constraint in healing, evidently, was not compassion—though such was included in His ministry—but rather the setting forth of His divine Person and power; and He sovereignly chose the time, place, method, people and individuals deemed best suited for this manifestation.

Christ was sovereign in the conditions which He imposed upon men as a means of physical healing. Teachers of miraculous healing usually state that several conditions must be fulfilled before healing may take place. These are expressed more or less as follows: first, one must be a Christian; second, one, if need be, must confess sin; third, one must be anointed with oil; fourth, one must more or less be holy in life; fifth, one must believe, not in general, but in particular, by putting one's faith in Christ as the Healer; sixth, one must accept healing; and lastly, one must act as if healed, believing that one is healed as one so acts. If all of these conditions are required, certainly healing will remain restricted to the few, for the many will not be capable of fulfilling them. In addition, if all of these conditions are required, it will always be easy to say that this or that person was not healed because he was not sufficiently holy or did not exercise the proper degree of faith. But aside from these objections to the long list of conditions given, where in God's Word will one find such an array of experiences and attainments as a requirement for healing?

If we take Christ's earthly ministry of healing as a standard, and, therefore, as an interpretation of miraculous healing, we are impressed by the discrepancy which exists between His practice and the above-mentioned conditions. First, Christ did not require that a man should be a disciple in order to be healed, as the case of the blind man attests (John 9:1, 17, 25, 35, 36), and the cases of the unevangelized multitudes who thronged upon Him suggest (Matt. 4:24; 14:35, 36; 15:30, 31; Mark 1:32–34; Luke 17:11–19); second, Christ did not always demand that a man should confess his sin before he could be healed, there being no such intimation in His general acts of healing (John 5:1–15; 9:17, 24, 25, 35–38); third, Christ, so far as we know, never anointed with oil, and yet He healed; fourth, Christ did not hold back healing until men had attained to holiness of life, but healed multitudes just as they were, in their spiritual ignorance and common-level living (Matt. 14:35, 36; Mark 1:33, 34; Luke 6:17–19; 8:49–56); and fifth, Christ seldom laid down the rule of a peculiar attainment of faith before healing was granted, but often responded to the simplest and most ignorant appeals (Mark 9:25–27). In other words, the requirements for healing expressed by miraculous healing teachers are not found in the practice of Christ. On the contrary, whether there was salvation or lack of salvation, holiness or absence of holiness, special faith or want of special faith, Christ dispensed His healing according to His sovereign grace and purpose. He was chiefly demonstrating His deity, and the healing of the unjust and spiritually undeveloped signified this as truly as that of the just and sanctified (Matt. 15:30, 31). And what was true of Christ's healings when He was on earth, has been true of His healings since He has been in heaven. In the apostolic days after Pentecost, men were healed who had hardly or not at all fulfilled the above conditions (Acts 3:1–8; 9:36–42; 19:11, 12; 28:7, 8); and during modern times, healings have taken place amongst those who have not been converted or have been in a primitive development of faith and holiness, as the history of missions in China and other foreign fields indisputably attests.

Christ was sovereign in the limitations which He put upon Himself in His acts of healing. It must be remembered that Christ, when He was on earth, possessed and exercised infinite power in respect to miracles. The stilling of the troubled waters of the lake of Galilee, the walking upon those waters, the feeding of five thousand persons with five loaves and two fishes and the raising of Lazarus from the grave when he had been four days dead, indicate that He could have done whatever He might have desired on behalf of the human body. Moreover, He made this power plain by miracles related to the body, such as restoring sight and hearing, straightening out deformed limbs and restoring men from leprosy, for He thus manifested the fact that He could have done anything and everything for the physical frame of man. But nothing in the Scriptures is plainer than this, that He did not do anything and everything. For instance, He did not lengthen out the lives of those He healed to the patriarchal age, making men live from two hundred to nine hundred years; nor did He anticipate the millennial condition when there will be no more an infant of days, nor an old man who has not filled his days, when the child will die an hundred years old (Isa. 65:20); nor did He deliver those who He healed from further infirmities, for all who were healed eventually sickened and died. In fact, the things which Christ did not do in His various acts of healing were as remarkable as those which He did do, considering His hatred of sickness and death, His longing to consummate His redemptive and resurrection work, and His full purpose of finally undoing once and forever the ravages of sin, not only as related to the spirit and soul, but also to the body. To restrain Himself thus was sovereignty indeed wherein He deliberately chose to do in part what He intended ultimately to do in whole, and thus in spite of what these would mean to the human race He let sickness and death hold sway over the suffering sons of men, including those who were and were to be His blood-bought disciples.

Christ was sovereign in healing only those who were in immediate contact with Him. There are two notable exceptions to this statement recorded in the Gospels: the first, that of the centurion who left his servant in his house at Capernaum, sought out Jesus in some other part of the city, asked for healing and went back home to find his servant well (Matt. 8:5–13; Luke 7:1–10); and the second, that of the nobleman who lived at Capernaum, had a son there lying at the point of death, met Jesus at Cana, which was about ten miles away, asked him to heal his boy, received a favourable response and went back to his house to learn from his servants that his son had recovered at the very hour Jesus had spoken (John 4:46–53). But these two exceptions are a remarkable confirmation of my statement. They indicate that Jesus *could* have healed at any time, at any place, at any distance throughout Palestine and the world, for time, place and distance were no more to Him then than they are now when He is healing throughout the world in spite of the fact that He is millions or billions of miles away. Yet the record of the Gospels is perfectly plain. Aside from the two cases given, He ceased to heal in a given place immediately He had gone forth from it, reserving His healings for some new place where He Himself would be. This meant that He left places where He had shown His healing power wholly destitute of further healings. It also meant that He left untouched with His healing power great reaches in Palestine and the world, which contained innumerable villages and cities with countless sick and dying inhabitants, to the common, unrelieved conditions of human life. It would be interesting to pursue this line of thought and seek to discover why the compassionate Christ took such a course. But this is aside from our present purpose. What we would point out is this, that Christ did so act and that the basic reason was that He sovereignly chose to do so.

Christ was sovereign as to the persons to whom He gave

the gift of healing. He chose the twelve apostles and imparted to them power to heal others (Mark 16:15-18); and later, He commissioned the seventy disciples and likewise empowered them to heal others (Luke 10:1-9). Thus, only eighty-two men were chosen to perform miracles of healing. Stephen, Philip, Barnabas and Paul were afterwards added to this company, which brought up the number to eighty-six. But it is to be noted that no women were given healing power. And again it is to be noted that no other men, as far as the record shows, were given such power. These last are remarkable facts, for the disciples rapidly multiplied in the apostolic days, especially after Pentecost, and there is no reason for believing that many of these later disciples did not have the same holy life and strong faith which the Twelve and Seventy had. The explanation of the disparity, therefore, is not to be found in a difference between the men—as if the twelve apostles and seventy disciples reached a peculiar quality and degree of sanctity and faith—but rather in their particular calling and office. But when this is admitted, we are brought face to face with Christ's sovereign acts in choosing the Twelve and Seventy, in enduing them with special power for miracle-working and in confirming through them the Word preached with signs following (Mark 16:19, 20; Acts 2:43; 5:12). This exclusiveness on Christ's part in selecting those who would work miracles does not mean that He has never, from apostolic days to these, chosen others to heal sick saints, for facts, and even modern facts, are against such a conclusion. But it does mean that sovereignty in selection was the prevailing law of Christ's life on earth and that it is of His life in heaven.

Christ was sovereign in making the Holy Spirit sovereign in His miracle administration. This statement is true in reference to all of the operations of the Spirit, inclusive of the experience where one would least expect it to be a fact, namely, in salvation (John 3:8). To prove that this is presently true in respect to miracle-working in general, including the gift of healing, I would quote the following verses: "God also bearing them witness, both with signs and wonders, and with diverse miracles, and gifts of the Holy Ghost, *according to his own will"* (Heb. 2:4); "God hath set some in the church, first apostles, secondarily prophets, thirdly teachers, after that miracles, then *gifts of healings,* helps, governments, diversities of tongues. Are all apostles? are all prophets? are all teachers? are all workers of miracles? *have all the gifts of healing?* do all speak with tongues? do all interpret? (1 Cor. 12:28-30); "Now there are diversities of gifts, but the same Spirit. And there are differences of administrations, but the same Lord. And there are diversities of operations, but it is the same God which worketh all in all. But the manifestation of the Spirit is given to every man to profit withall. For to one is given by the Spirit the word of wisdom; to another the word of knowledge by the same Spirit; to another faith by the same Spirit; to another the *gifts of healing* by the same Spirit; to another the working of miracles; to another prophecy; to another discerning of spirits; to another diverse kinds of tongues; to another the interpretation of tongues: but all these worketh that one and the selfsame Spirit, *dividing to every man severally as he will"* (1 Cor. 12:4-11). Here, manifestly, we are informed that the Holy Spirit dispenses His miracle-gifts wholly and exclusively as He chooses. Once more, then, we are brought face to face with Christ's sovereignty in His healing operations. This last consideration is peculiarly important as it brings us to present times and into present experiences.

A remarkable example of Christ's power in working miracles and His sovereignty in the display of this power is given in Revelation 11:3-12. In this passage there is told the story of the two witnesses—possibly Moses and Elijah—who live in the last days and testify against the Antichrist and his followers. Christ's miracle-power is manifested in the mighty acts performed by these two witnesses, who "have power to shut heaven that it rain not in the days of their prophecy, and have power over waters to turn them to blood, and smite the earth with all plagues, as often as they will." And Christ's sovereignty is manifested in the way He deals with the two witnesses: first, in empowering them to perform such miracles as utterly overwhelmed their enemies; then, in allowing them to be overcome and killed, their dead bodies lying in the streets of Jerusalem and being made a spectacle to all; and finally, in raising them from death to heaven in a cloud, their enemies beholding them as they went up. Here in quick succession, as related to the same individuals, one sees Christ passing from one episode to another, with each experience different from and opposite to the other. In short, He does what He pleases with His two saints. And the two witnesses had no misunderstanding of Christ and expressed no objection to His ways. Whether used or not used, whether well or sick, whether living or dead, it was all the same to them, for they were prepared to follow the Lamb whithersoever He might go.

X

VARIOUS DEDUCTIONS

IF any one who has read the foregoing pages has concluded that I do not believe in miraculous healing, he has altogether misunderstood the purpose of my writing. It is true that I have sought to eliminate from my reader's thought what I believe are unwarranted theories and conclusions. But apart from this, it has been my intention to strengthen conviction to the effect that God can, does, and will heal, and also, that He will sometimes choose to keep from sickness so that healing will not be necessary. Some godly men, such as Dr. Gordon and Dr. Simpson, were persons whose lives illustrated both of these facts, for they were frequently healed and generally they were granted such good health as enabled them to accomplish almost unbelievably hard tasks through many years. And not a few others of God's serving children, such as Dr Cullis, have had either the same or a somewhat similar experience.

Paul said to King Agrippa, "Why should it be thought a thing incredible with you that God should raise the dead?" (Acts 26:8). And I would say to my reader, If you believe that God can raise the dead, why should it be thought a thing incredible with you that He should heal and care for the body? The greater always includes the lesser. Manifestly, then, if God can raise a new and living body from an old and dead one, He can heal a body which is new and not old, living and not dead. We need to have confidence in the power of God in respect to our mortal frames, being assured that He is greater than we think. Let us lay it to heart that Christ is still a miracle-worker, with as much power as when He went about on earth healing all manner of sickness and all manner of disease (Matt. 4:23). As long as we give Him the ultimate right of choice, and are as submissive and thankful to Him when He says, No, as when He says, Yes, we may freely urge our physical claims upon Him, and this with much expectation. There are many saints who are not well and many others who are not strong, simply because they have never asked God to be their physical sufficiency. This is a sad plight for a Christian to be in, and it would seem as if such a person must be a great disappointment to the heart of God.

I know a minister who is not large or strong, and who holds no particular theory about divine healing beyond that of looking to God for health and strength. He is almost constantly preaching or teaching, is frequently travelling, is daily bearing heavy administrative burdens, is often drawing heavily upon his sympathies as he gives help to those who are spiritually needy, and is fulfilling his tasks with clear mind and almost undiminished physical vigour. He is all this at the advanced age of nearly eighty years. Let us grant that this friend is an exception to divine rules and even divine grace. Nevertheless, we may regard him as an example of what God, when He pleases, can do for our mortal bodies, especially if we live in dependence upon Him. There is infinite meaning in that little word, "The Lord for the body" (I Cor. 6:13). It opens up to us a vista of divine power, love, compassion and care such as most of us have never dreamed of. We need to pray, therefore, that we may not miss privileges which possibly God has for us.

To me it is a blessed experience, if sickness has come, not to turn first to a physician, but rather to God; to put myself wholly at His disposal, either for sickness or health; to enquire what He would have me do in seeking for healing; to ask, if the circumstances suggest this, that He will heal miraculously; to seek, lacking such healing, to know His mind in respect to healing of some other sort; and finally to accept the issue of His will, whatever it may be, not only submissively, but also in trust and with praise. This order of procedure, it seems to me, is a happy one for the saint to take, because it puts God first, gives Him opportunity to work and gives Him the right-of-way all through. In taking a course like this, sometimes God has healed me miraculously; and, if not, has either used in my behalf the physician and his medicine, or given me extra grace to welcome and endure the sickness. As touching this last, it is to be remembered that the Word not only says, "The Lord for the body," but also, "The body for the Lord" (1 Cor. 6:13); and, if I mistake not, this indicates that our bodies are to be put and kept at God's disposal for whatever He may choose for them.

I have said in the preceding pages that compassion for the bodies of men was not the main motive which moved Christ, when He was on earth, to dispense healing to those who were in physical need. This, it seems to me, is a statement which may be established from the Word. But granting that the statement is true, it must not be concluded that compassion was not *a* motive in moving Christ to heal. It is said again and again, in respect to His various acts of healing, "He was moved with compassion on them" (Matt. 9:36; 14:14; 18:27; 29:34. Mark 1:41; 5:19. Luke 7:13; 10:33). Also, it must not be concluded that Christ had compassion upon the needy sons of men when He was on earth, but has no such compassion now that He is in heaven. Christ is the eternal Son of God, and He is in His divine attributes, "the same yesterday and to-day and forever" (Heb. 13:8). If, therefore, He loved in the days of His flesh, He loves now; if He cared then, He cares now; if He healed then, He will undoubtedly heal now. It does not necessarily follow that He will do now all that He did then, or that He will do what He does now in the same way as He did then, for His purposes in some things are different at present from what they were in the past. Nevertheless, Christ is changeless in character, and we may be sure that He is infinitely interested in us and concerned about us. Even the stern and rugged James saw the above truth, and from his lips fell this most comforting word, "Ye have . . . seen the end of the Lord, that the Lord is very pitiful and of tender mercy" (Jas. 5:11). Christ has many things to think of in planning for a saint; He must have in mind what is best for the individual; what is the greatest profit in respect to his testimony; what is required in his relationship to many other saints; and what is to make most for God's present and eternal glory; and He will hold resolutely, in answering prayer, to that course which will combine in bringing the largest and most enduring good to pass. At the same time, He will never deny Himself (2 Tim. 2:13); He will have compassion upon whom He will have compassion (Rom. 9:15); He will be touched with the feeling of our infirmities (Heb. 4:15); He will ever be the faithful Creator (1 Pet. 4:19); He will desire our bodies to prosper as certainly and as much as our souls do (3 John 2); He will encourage us to pray if we are afflicted (Jas. 5:13); and He will answer prayer, even in the lesser things of life, if He sees it is right to do so (1 Thes. 5:17; Phil. 4:6; 1 Pet. 5:7). Let us, then, not say, God cannot heal and will not do so. Let us rather say, God can heal and He will do so if it is for His glory.

I have also said in the preceding pages that Christ's chief motive, when He was on earth and healing men, was the proclaiming of the fact that He was the promised Messiah, the Son of God. This statement, too, it seems to me, may be substantiated from the Word. In addition, I have stated that there was the lesser need of healing-miracles after the New Testament had been written than before, since Christ's earthly acts and divine claims were therein set forth. This statement also, it seems to me, may be substantiated from the Word. Let us grant, then, that the two affirmations are true. But does it necessarily follow that there is no further necessity of proving by signs of healing that Jesus is indeed the Christ, the everlasting Son of the Father?

In answering this question, two great facts are to be kept in mind: first, in the greater part of the world and amongst the largest number of peoples the Bible has never been circulated and the missionary may make no appeal to it; and second, among Christianized peoples the apostasy of modernism has greatly undermined confidence in the authenticity of the Scriptures, so that the preacher's appeal to it is largely non-effective. The first of these facts brings us face to face with the condition which prevailed in Christ's day as a result of non-enlightenment; and the second forces us to confront a similar condition as a result of unbelief. It is, therefore, true that there are large parts of the world where healing-miracles, in proof of a living and all-powerful Christ, may well be looked for; and it may confidently be anticipated, as the present apostasy increases, that Christ will manifest His deity and lordship in increasing measure through miracle-signs, including healings. We are not to say, therefore, that the Word is sufficient. It is so to those who know and believe it; but it is not so to those who have never heard of it, or who, having heard, have disbelieved it. To these persons, a dramatic appeal may have to be made, and on the plane where such will most easily be understood, namely, the physical. The missionary abroad, therefore, may have it in mind, in a case of the sickness of others, that God may choose to make him a miracle-worker; and the worker at home may understand that He may choose to make some sick saint, as He made the apostles, a spectacle, or—as it reads literally—a "theatre unto the world, and to angels, and to men" (1 Cor. 4:9). And what true child of God will not be willing to be used by Him in these ways, as in any and every other? It is our privilege then, in respect to ourselves, to present our bodies unto God, as a living sacrifice, for this is our reasonable service (Rom. 12:1). After an utter surrender of this kind, it will be for the all-wise Christ to determine how we may most glorify Him, whether by life or death, whether by health or sickness, whether by miracle or non-miracle. If, therefore, I understand God and His Word aright, I may confidently say that not infrequently for such an one, in case of sickness, God will set forth the fact, by a miracle-sign of healing, that there is a priest at His right hand of His own choosing (Heb. 5:5–10), and that in Him dwelleth all the fullness of the godhead bodily (Col. 1:15–19). Of such an One we need have no fear, since perfect love casteth out fear (1 John 4:18); and upon such an One we may cast all our care, for He careth for us (1 Pet. 5:7).

It is never to be forgotten that the death of Christ on Calvary's cross opened wide the floodgates of God's love to all of His dear children. God always loved; but our sin had fast closed to us the gates of His stored-up love in Christ. When, however, Christ had put away sin by the sacrifice of Himself (Heb. 9:16), then those gates were flung wide open and love was poured forth upon us in a very torrent (Rom. 8:32). Thenceforth, God's love was more than a love of compassion; it was also a love of friendship, companionship and fellowship. Even in the Old Testament times, in view of the atonement, God gave such a love to His chosen and faithful children. God said of Abraham, His friend, "Shall I hide from Abraham that thing that I do?" (Gen. 18:17); and to Daniel He said, "O man greatly beloved; fear not; peace be unto thee" (Dan. 10:19). Again in New Testament times He poured out His tenderest love for His chosen ones. Christ took Peter and James and John into the mount and was there transfigured before them (Matt. 17:1, 2); the Spirit gave to John an open-eyed vision of the risen and glorified Christ (Rev. 1:12-17); and Christ vouchsafed to Paul to be caught up into Paradise and to hear there unspeakable words, which it is not lawful for a man to utter (2 Cor. 12:4). These episodes betoken intimacies of the closest kind, wherein heart went out to heart and confidence to confidence.

It was to such men that God revealed Himself as the great miracle-worker. It is not difficult to understand why God let Abraham live to a ripe old age (Gen. 25.7), or why He touched Daniel when he was sick and raised him up (Dan. 8:27; 10:18, 19); or why He gave Peter and John the gift of healing (Acts 3:1-8); or why He revived Paul when he was stoned and left for dead (Acts 14:19, 20), and also why He gave him the gift of healing (Acts 14:8 10; 20:9 12). We must admit that these were special miracles, and hence special experiences. Nevertheless, they were God's tokens of trust and love to those who lived peculiarly near to Himself, and they establish the principle that He delights to manifest His power to those who are worthy of receiving and using it. We ought not to be surprised, therefore, if some of the miracle-power which flows from Calvary's cross, reaches us and bears us onward to ocean depths and breadths of experience. I do not consider healing, with or without means, God's highest expression of love and trust. I believe rather, that ordained or permitted suffering is this (Heb. 12:6; 2 Tim 2:12). At the same time, healing is *an* expression of love and trust, and one of a very tender kind. We may be confident, therefore, that close companionship and fellowship with God will ensure to us beautiful and blessed surprises of grace, wherein He will make great use of us, wherein Christ will not suffer us to be tempted above that we are able (2 Cor. 10:13), and wherein His deliverances will include, at such times and in such measure as His love will choose and grant, good health, and, when health has failed, miraculous healing.

I have been deeply impressed, from time to time, with the word of the Apostle Paul in 1 Corinthians 15:45. In the Authorised Version it reads: "The first Adam was made a living soul; the last Adam was made a quickening spirit." In the Revised Version it reads, "The first man, Adam, became a living soul. The last Adam became a life-giving spirit." Reading literally from the Greek we can phrase the words thus: "The first man, Adam, became a living soul; the last Adam a vitalizing spirit." Now, whichever of these translations we may choose, the words are remarkable. First, they signify that the first Adam was a creature, and that the last Adam was a Creator. Second, they declare that the first Adam received life, and that the last Adam gave life. Third, they imply that the first Adam, being a creature, may never rise above the creature's position, but that the last Adam, being the Creator, ever remains what He was in the act of primal creation. And lastly, they assert that the first Adam is a living one, while the last Adam was, is, and ever will be a life-giving or vitalizing One. This last thought brings us to the fact that Christ is a constant life-giver and hence connects the passage with our subject. It means that all men live, move, and have their being in God (Acts 17:28). And it signifies that this is particularly true of the Christian, for it is he who is indwelt by the Holy Spirit and who has his life in Christ (1 Cor. 3:16; Col. 3:4). In the face of these facts, what cannot Christ do, within the limit of His will, for one who is unreservedly His own? He can appoint him, like Paul, to the extreme of suffering; and that one will accept the appointment without cavil and with joy and praise (2 Cor. 4:7–12). Or, He can appoint him to healing, to continued health and strength, and to vigorous work and length of days; and that one will accept his appointment with thanksgiving and use all that is given him to the glory of God (Eph. 2:1–13). What a glorious title of Christ it is for needy saints to keep in mind and depend upon—"The vitalizing Spirit." This our Lord is and is ready to be, to the degree of our need and the measure of His ever blessed will concerning us.

There are two words which would bring to me the assurance that God, from time to time, will give healing to His children, even if there was not another word in the Bible concerning the matter. I refer to the Lord's prayer and the words, "Our Father" (Matt. 6:9). I have a son who is a physician. His young daughter, not long since, was seriously sick. The doctor-father at the time had many professional cares upon him and was very busy. I noticed, however, that he did not give himself to his outside duties without reference to his child. On the contrary, he turned from these to her, and with brooding care brought all his skill to bear in seeking for her recovery until she was past all danger and was well. And do we imagine that an earthly physician who is a father will show such solicitude concerning his child and the heavenly Father remain indifferent concerning His? "If ye then, being evil, know how to give good gifts unto your children, how *much more* shall your Father which is in heaven give good things to them that ask him" (Matt. 7:11). And surely, when a saint is sick and health and strength are needed for the maintaining of his service and the obtaining of the glory of God, healing, and possibly miraculous healing, is a *very* good thing. About all, therefore, that a child of God needs to do in a time of sickness, is to lie quite still and breathe into God's ear the words, "My Father!" After this, he may surely expect "good gifts," and oftentimes may look for great and even miraculous ones.

XI

GENERAL CONCLUSIONS

In this chapter I desire to present the conclusions which I have reached, on the basis of the thoughts presented in the foregoing chapters, in reference to the Christian's privilege in respect to miraculous healing and strengthening. In doing this, in view of the difficulty of the subject, I shall not dogmatize. I shall abstain, therefore, from seeking to lay down rules for any person. The most that I shall do will be to state the spiritual principles, in reference to the body, which have governed and do govern my own life. As to whether or not these represent the teaching of God's inspired Word and thus are to be adopted and followed, the reader must be the judge. The following, then, are my personal views:

Christ's atoning work, His resurrection, His ascension and His pouring forth of the Holy Spirit brought to the church on earth great and wonderful privileges.

One of the results of Christ's redemption and intercession is to bring the saint into intimate relationship with Himself, which may include, so far as the saint's consciousness is concerned, a life of constant obedience and uninterrupted communion.

As a consequence of this intimate relationship and fellowship, the Lord is to be recognized as having the right-of-way over the life of the saint, so that He may do what He wills with him—as in the cases of the apostles—whether this be for physical weal or woe.

Christ will always remain sovereign in His dealings with His saint, not ruthlessly but lovingly and tenderly, with His glory and the fulfillment of His purposes in view, and also, the best interests of His child, and this for time and eternity.

Christ will choose health, strength and length of days for some of His saints; He will choose the opposite for others of them. Also, He may choose opposite experiences for the same saint at different times.

When a saint is well, it is his bounden duty, being a bond-slave of Christ, to use all of his physical, mental and spiritual powers for the praise and glory of his Saviour and Lord.

When a saint is sick, the same obligation, within the limit of his strength, is upon him; and he has the additional obligation, in order to test and discover God's will concerning him, of seeking to re-obtain the health which he has lost.

The saint, in doing this last, has three possible courses divinely set before him; first, he may seek healing through a physician and his treatment; or second, without a physician and his ministry, but through rest and change of scene and occupation; or third, without a physician and without rest and change, and through God alone.

It is to be recognized that all of the three kinds of healing referred to are divine healings, God alone being the creator, maintainer and healer of the body. It is to be further recognized that the last named kind of healing—which is properly miraculous healing—is no more divine than the two healings first named, all being of God and all manifesting Him, the only difference between miraculous healing and healing through means being this, that miraculous healing more fully demonstrates the divine presence and power.

Miraculous healing may be tested and discovered by applying to each supposed case the New Testament conditions of such, where the healings were always immediate, complete and final. If these conditions do not pertain to a given case of healing, then it is divine healing, but it is not miraculous healing.

In seeking for healing the saint is to have regard to the nature of the disease with which he is afflicted. If this is entirely within the scope of man's ability to give aid, it—apart from special guidance to the contrary—would be unlawful to set aside what God has graciously provided, and hence, recourse is to be had to a physician. If it does not call for medical assistance, and rest and change will be sufficient, then again it would be unlawful to set aside these divinely appointed means, and restoration is to be sought by rest at home, exercise outside, going to the mountains or seaside, etc. If it is of such a nature that means of any sort and all sorts are valueless, then God may be appealed to in the hope and confidence that He may do what man and natural processes have failed to do and cannot do. In all three of these methods, prayer and faith are to be exercised, as, whether means are or are not used, it is God alone who heals.

In the case of a saint meeting with accident and needing immediate physical attention, it is right that friends at hand should give first-aid treatment and that a surgeon should be sent for, since God has given to friends and surgeons the skill to use in such emergencies. But in case the treatment given fails, again appeal may be made to God to do what man cannot do.

God, judging from the Scripture and experience, may possibly put forth miraculous power and heal apart from means under the following circumstances: first, when, from the beginning, the disease is of such a nature as to make all known means valueless; second, when it is impossible—as sometimes occurs upon the mission field—to secure medical aid; third, when medical men have attempted to bring healing to pass and have failed to do so; fourth, where a servant of God has a divinely appointed task set before him which some ailment hinders his fulfilling, where this task must immediately be performed and where there is neither time nor opportunity to have recourse to usual means; fifth, where a missionary is labouring in unevangelized parts and the Bible, because uncirculated and unknown, cannot be appealed to, and where a miracle is needed to prove God's existence and the missionary's divine appointment; and lastly, where God indicates, whether at home or abroad, that there is need of giving a new demonstration of His presence and power in proof that He is the living and loving Father in heaven.

The saint is to remember, in all the foregoing conditions, that God is the judge as to whether or not He will display Himself and His power by a miraculous act, and also when, where, how, and with whom this will be done; and he is to keep constantly in mind that God is just as faithful and loving when He does not so display Himself as when He does.

The saint is ever to remain submissive to God's will, whatever this may mean. But also, he is to be assured that he has a Father in heaven, that He is very pitiful and of tender mercy, that He will not willingly afflict, and that He is more willing to give good gifts to His children than earthly parents are to theirs.

The Christian, for these reasons, while not going back to Old Testament positions and not attempting to appropriate Jewish or even apostolic promises, may understand that God, at times, will be pleased to respond to faith and prayer, to put forth His miraculous power, and to heal disease, especially such as is otherwise incurable.

It is, therefore, the Christian's right, particularly if human help has failed and a physical crisis has come, to offer prayer and exercise faith, and thus to give God the opportunity to prove Himself to be the faithful Creator and the Lord of the body.

It is sometimes God's choice, when He has called one to a special service, to keep that one, in general, from sickness and maintain him in health and strength, and hence, it is the privilege of such a saint, until his task has been accomplished, to look to God for the continual renewing of his physical life. But even such a saint as this is to look forward —the Lord tarrying—to the inevitable end of sickness and death, and be prepared, at last, to welcome such without misunderstanding his heavenly Father and hence in a spirit of faith, joy and praise.

XII

A CLOSING TESTIMONY

In confirmation of what I have before said that God, when His time has come, can and often does grant miraculous healing, I would subjoin the following experience out of our family life.

In the year 1908, our family consisted of Mrs. Frost, seven children and myself. We lived in Germantown, Philadelphia, in the Home of the China Inland Mission, at 235 School Lane. God had richly favoured us as a family, our children, with us, being Christians and all of us having the best of health. Separately and unitedly our hearts were full of thanksgiving to Him, for we were enjoying His daily blessing in all things.

In the early part of August of that year, the members of the family were somewhat separated from one another. The two older boys, the three girls and I were at Attica, in western New York, and our next to the youngest son was visiting friends nearer home. This left Mrs. Frost and our youngest child alone at Germantown. I had gone away to obtain change and rest, for the heavy work of the Mission and the excessive summer heat at Germantown had brought me into a low physical condition and there was need of recuperation.

In spite of our separation and my indisposition, our family affairs were going on smoothly and happily enough. This remained true until we reached the middle of the month. Then on the 18th, a sad calamity befell us. Our youngest child F., a boy of five years, met with a severe accident. He was playing in the dining-room of the Germantown Home, passed through a swinging door into the adjoining butler's pantry, climbed up a number of shelves of the china pantry to get a cup on the top shelf, lost his hold as he reached for it, pitched backward, fell down about seven feet and struck the back and right side of his head on the hard, wooden floor below. The maid, at the time, was setting the table in the dining-room for luncheon. She heard the fall, ran into the pantry, found the boy lying unconscious, picked him up, carried him upstairs and laid him in his mother's arms, he having revived as he was borne up the stairs. Mrs. Frost laid him on the bed of a back bedroom and telephoned for Dr. R., our Christian physician. This friend was away from home, as was the case with other physicians whom she called. Dr. R. returned after four days, found F. in fair condition—though he had been very sick—advised quiet and rest, and expressed the conviction that all would be well.

Mrs. Frost sent the above report to me at Attica. It was, of course, a startling tale and my instinct was to return at once to Germantown. But Dr. Ellinwood, Mrs. Frost's father, in whose medical care I was, practically forbade my going back to the heat of that place in the physical state in which I was, and besides, Mrs. Frost soon assured me that I was to have no anxiety concerning F. I stayed on, therefore, at Attica, and Mrs. Frost had the care of her child. I came to know afterwards that she finally, not wishing to call me home, held back from me the news that certain serious symptoms had developed. The result was that I remained away two weeks longer. Dr. R. then, as F.'s condition had become serious, insisted upon her telegraphing for me. I started at once for Germantown, arriving there on September 5th. I found on arrival that our child could take little food, was having chills, was running high temperatures, had to be kept, for the most part, in a deeply darkened room, and was suffering from severe pain in the head, which generally lasted, with short intervals between, as long as ten hours. It was evident that Dr. R. was not only much concerned, but also greatly perplexed. He thought that F. was suffering from meningitis. But there were complications which he did not understand.

Matters having reached this crisis, Dr. R. told us that he had decided to call in for consultation Dr. B. and Dr. S., who were two of Philadelphia's most notable physicians. Dr. S. came once and Dr. B twice, and they and Dr. R. spent hours examining F., in the endeavour to discover what special form of disease was afflicting him. After the second examination by Dr. R. and Dr. B. they asked to see me privately. Dr. B. then spoke as follows:

"Mr. Frost, Dr. R. and I are agreed that F. is suffering from meningitis. We have also concluded that it is probable that an abscess on the brain has formed, beneath the place where he struck. We have concluded, therefore, to advise an operation being performed, namely, trephining the skull. It is for you to decide whether or not this shall be done."

I felt, before I could reach a conclusion, that I needed information, and so I said:

"Dr. B., what chance is there of F. getting well as he is now?"

Dr. B. replied, "None whatever."

"What," I exclaimed, "is the boy dying?"

"Well," said the doctor, "he may last some days; but he will not recover."

"Then," said I, "what chance is there of his getting well if an operation is performed?"

The doctor thought a moment or two and then answered, "I am, of course, not sure, but I should say about one in ten."

This word was staggering. No chance as F. was, and only one in ten if he were to be operated on! What should I decide? I silently thought and prayed. At last I said,

"Thank you, Dr. B., for your frankness; I'll take the one chance in ten."

The interview with the physicians had taken place on Saturday morning, September 19th, and on the evening of that day we took F. in a comfortable carriage to the Germantown Hospital. There I left him, Mrs. Frost remaining with him, with the understanding that he would be operated on by Dr. S. the next noon. Dr. R. and Dr. B. promised to be present.

Our two older boys had returned to Germantown and they accompanied me, the next morning, to the Hospital. Both boys were a comfort to us. This was particularly true of our second son, who, at the time, was studying medicine. He was a comfort to F. also, and, when the time for the operation came, carried the little fellow from the private room, down the long corridor, into the operating room, where he left him with the three doctors and the nurses. The operation began at 12 and ended at 12.50. Following this, Dr. R. and Dr. B. came to the outside veranda, where Mrs. Frost, the two boys and I were waiting, with the kind purpose of reporting to us the result. Dr. R. took the lead in speaking. He said,

"Mr. Frost, the operation is over and it has been successful; but we have found no abscess and we are just where we were before."

I did then, in the strain of the moment, an impetuous and somewhat rude thing. I exclaimed,

"Thank God! Now we know exactly where we are; it is God or no one!"

"Yes," said good Dr. R., "you are quite right; it is God or no one."

F. was taken back to his room. We later saw him there, his eyes closed, his face ashy white and his head enveloped with a bandage which left to view only the oval of his face. It was a pathetic sight, and also a hopeless one.

Following this, there began a long fight for life. The boy could take no solid food, or, if he did, could not retain it, and thus what little strength and flesh were left were wasting away. The burden of nursing fell on Mrs. Frost, for F. cried piteously for her if she left his side. One day his mother said to him,

"F., isn't there *anything* you would like to eat?"

"Yes," the boy feebly answered, "corn flakes."

I turned to the house doctor standing by and asked,

"Shall we try them?"

The doctor did not reply, but simply shrugged his shoulders, meaning, "You can try them if you will, but they will do no good." We did try them, and to our surprise the lad enjoyed the food and retained it. This led to some improvement and gave us slight hope, and, on October 3rd, it was possible for the Hospital ambulance to take us, with our dear boy, to our home on School Lane. We had been greatly touched, during the long sickness, by the sympathy which had been expressed by persons who knew or did not know us, the whole community being moved by our son's sufferings. Among those who inquired were many physicians in Philadelphia who, largely because of professional interest in the case, telephoned to ask how the boy was. We were specially touched, about this time, to learn that, on the Sunday morning of the operation, F. had been publicly prayed for in six of the Germantown churches. So our son was laid in his bed at home, and we resumed our anxious watch at his side.

The days which followed were terrible ones. Formerly, the chills, fever and headache had occurred every day. Now, they occurred every other day. But the temperature would rise as high as 103 degrees, and once it stood at 105.[1] This meant that the severity of the attacks had greatly increased. When they came on, F. would soon be in paroxysms of pain, crying out over and over again, "Oh mother, my head hurts, my head hurts!" At such times, all that Dr. R. could do was to give him opiates; all that the mother could do was to keep cold compresses upon the aching head and hold the fevered hand; and all that I could do was to take my turn in watching or stand aside and pray. A hundred, a thousand times, now that the doctors had failed and a spirit of hopelessness was prevailing, we pleaded with God to come to our help and heal. But no answer was given. The poor boy grew steadily worse and he seemed doomed to die. One Sunday about the middle of November F. seemed a little better. It was an off day when the fever was not likely to recur, so Mrs. Frost dressed her boy and carried him out to the sitting-room that he might have a change of environment. Then, as Mrs. Frost and I had not been at church for many weeks, we ventured out to the morning service at Westside Church, which was only a block and a half away. As we had left our son in the care of his eldest brother, who by his tender ways had a wonderfully soothing influence upon him, we felt confident that all would be well. But as we were returning along School Lane we heard the dreaded cries. We ran into the house and up the stairs and there we found F. undressed and back in bed and in a terrible spasm of pain. Thereupon Mrs. Frost

---

[1] The physicians found that it was not a case of malaria.

took her place at her child's side, and for eighteen long
dreadful hours we watched over that pain-racked form. At
last, at six o'clock in the morning, the poor lad, from sheer
exhaustion, fell into a deep sleep. We ourselves then lay down
on our bed, and we too fell asleep. We slept till about nine
o'clock, when we rose and dressed. Later, our son wakened
and wanted to get up. Mrs. Frost dressed him and took him
into the sitting-room.

It was now four months since F. had received his injury.
As many as twelve physicians had seen him, and all, including
the specialists, had confessed that the disease was beyond
their understanding and power to heal. This had led to much
prayer on the part of our friends and ourselves. Many of our
friends were praying earnestly that God Himself would heal
our son; but all of these were left in a state of doubt. Mrs.
Frost and I renewed our prayers for divine interposition; but
we received no assurance that God would heal. As I look back
on those days and call to remembrance our spiritual experiences, I can bear witness to the fact that we did not once
doubt God's love and compassion and His ability to give
miraculous healing. At the same time, I have to confess that
mentally and physically we were utterly exhausted. This last
was the case even with courageous Mrs. Frost, for she had
been seriously strained by long watching at the sick bed.
She had been awake night after night. Also, she had sat
beside our son, stroking his head or holding his hand, through
many a long, weary day, and this in a darkened room, where
the outer shutters were closed and the inner shades drawn,
since the least ray of light pierced the boy's eyes and brain
as red-hot needles might have done. And here, at the end
of these months, there was no improvement and the doctors
had, as it were, been forced to abandon our son and ourselves.
Our state, therefore, was one of helplessness and it bordered
on hopelessness. It was just then a wonderful thing took
place.

Mrs. Frost on the day to which we had come had hope of
a short respite, for, the temperature having risen the day
before, she concluded, according to the remittent form of the
disease, that it would not rise on that day. But at eleven

o'clock in the morning she saw that F. was in one of his preliminary chills, that his face was white and drawn and that the fever was beginning to recur. This was almost beyond my wife's physical .endurance. She stood, therefore, looking at her boy in a sort of daze. Suddenly, a divine impulse seized her. She took F. by the hand, said to him, "Come with me," led him to her darkened bedroom, closed the door, knelt with her beloved child beside the bed and cried,

"O dear Father in heaven, I can never go through this again! Please don't let him ever have another headache!"

And he never did. The sovereign and compassionate Lord, having brought us to an end of all human resources, had, at last, chosen to heal. Instantly, the chills, fever and headache passed away. From thence onward, he was able to take and retain food in a perfectly normal way. He put on flesh and weight and increased in strength. He was dressed day by day and was soon playing indoors and out as a well child might do. From that time to this there has never been a suspicion of his old trouble. In 1922, when he was nineteen years of age, he was a freshman at Princeton University, at which time he was examined by the Physical Director of the University and rated as in class A, which meant that he was in excellent physical condition. In the next years, he was a member of the tennis squad and one of the pitchers on the Varsity baseball nine. He is now in business, alert in mind, vigorous in action and physically fit and strong. In other words, his recovery bore all of the marks of a New Testament healing, that is, it was instantaneous, complete and permanent. It was, therefore, miraculous. When I next saw Dr. R., I told him of F.'s recovery, and added,

"I guess, doctor, we may conclude that God did it."

"Yes," replied the Christian doctor, "there is no doubt of it; God did it!"

And all the community at Germantown agreed with us, for those who were Christians and those who were not were constrained to acknowledge that a great and notable miracle had been wrought in their midst.

Our son's healing demonstrates the fact that God's choices are wisest, His times best, His ways perfect and His love and compassion infinite. Also, it proclaims the fact that Jesus Christ is the living Son of God and that He still has power on earth, not only to forgive sin, but also to heal disease. I would state it then, as my closing testimony in this book, that it is my conviction that God will readily answer our prayers for bodily healing; and I would add that it also is my conviction that if He defers answering or gives no answer at all, it is not because He does not love or care or desire to heal, but only because He has some better thing in store for us which time or eternity will reveal. Thus I would affirm that I am ever increasingly persuaded that, whether in health or sickness, life or death, we may trust our heavenly Father with an utter abandonment of confidence, being assured of the fact that—

"They who trust Him wholly
Find Him wholly true!"

"Now unto him that is able to do
exceeding
abundantly
above all
that we ask or think,
according to the power that worketh in us,
unto him
be glory in the church
by Christ Jesus
throughout all ages,
world without end:
Amen!"